FOUNDER

Also by Amos Elon

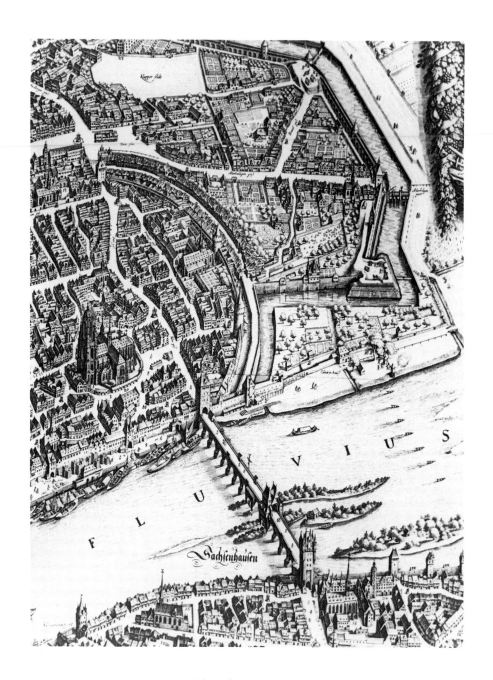

Plan of Frankfurt, 1628.

FOUNDER

Meyer Amschel Rothschild
and his Time

AMOS ELON

HarperCollins*Publishers*

HarperCollins*Publishers*
77–85 Fulham Palace Road
Hammersmith, London, w6 8jb

Published by HarperCollins*Publishers* 1996
1   3   5   7   9   8   6   4   2

Copyright © Amos Elon 1996

Amos Elon has asserted the moral right to
be identified as the author of this work

ISBN 0 00 255706-1

Set in Postscript Janson by
Rowland Phototypesetting Limited
Bury St Edmunds, Suffolk

Printed in Great Britain by
The Bath Press
Bath

Riches cover a multitude of woes

Menander, *The Boaetian Girl*

CONTENTS

ACKNOWLEDGEMENTS

This is not an 'authorized' or 'official' biography. Nevertheless, in researching and writing this book I have had such a great degree of encouragement and support from several members of the Rothschild family in England and France, and from the staff of the Rothschild Archive in London, that it is difficult for me to make adequate acknowledgements of all of them. Mr Victor Gray and Ms Melanie Aspey of the Rothschild Archive spared no energy to make available the remaining material on Meyer Amschel Rothschild and his sons, as did Mr Georg Heuberger, Mr Fritz Backhaus and Ms Helga Krohn at the Frankfurt Jewish Museum. Mr Arthur Fried of Jerusalem gave generously of his time to clarify to the layman a few of the more arcane corners of international finance. The private archive of the Vienna branch of the Rothschild family that was confiscated by the Nazis in 1938 was transported in 1945 to Moscow where it is now available, though not without some difficulties, at the Ozoby Arkhiv. I am indebted to the staff of this archive as well as to that of the Archives Nationales in Paris, the Bavarian and Marburg State and the Frankfurt City Archives, which I was able to consult. Thanks are also due to the Frankfurt Jewish Museum and the Historical Museum of Frankfurt for permission to reproduce the contemporary illustrations that appear in this volume. I am also indebted to my English editor Stuart Proffitt, who laboured over this text, and to Toby Mundy, whose meticulous attention to detail proved invaluable in preparing the manuscript for the printer.

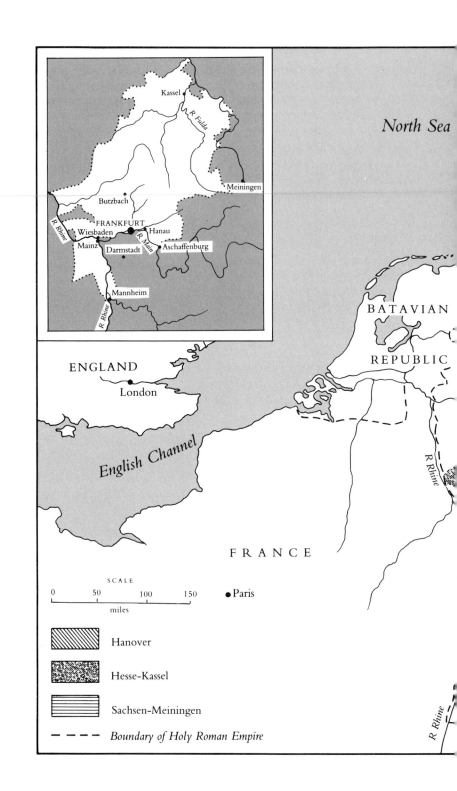

North Sea

Kassel

R. Fulda

Meiningen

Butzbach

FRANKFURT
Wiesbaden   Hanau
R. Rhine   R. Main
Mainz   Darmstadt   Aschaffenburg

Mannheim

R. Rhine

BATAVIAN

REPUBLIC

ENGLAND

London

R. Rhine

English Channel

FRANCE

SCALE

0   50   100   150   ● Paris

miles

Hanover

Hesse-Kassel

Sachsen-Meiningen

– – – –   Boundary of Holy Roman Empire

R. Rhine

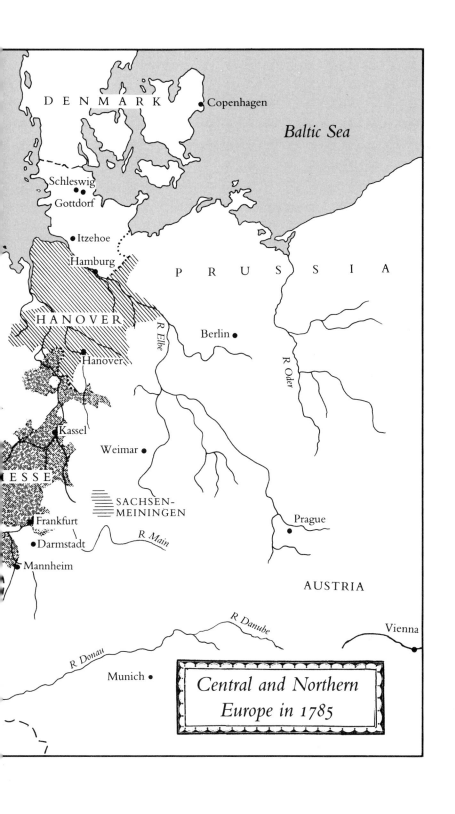

DENMARK

Copenhagen •

Baltic Sea

• Schleswig
• Gottdorf

• Itzehoe

Hamburg •

P   R   U   S   S   I   A

HANOVER

R Elbe

Berlin •

R Oder

• Hanover

Kassel •

Weimar •

ESSE

SACHSEN-
MEININGEN

Prague •

• Frankfurt

R Main

• Darmstadt

• Mannheim

AUSTRIA

R Danube

Vienna •

R Donau

Munich •

Central and Northern
Europe in 1785

LIST OF ILLUSTRATIONS

A NOTE ON PURCHASING POWER

In 1814, £1 was equivalent to 10 gulden, 20 francs or 5 thaler. Consumer prices have risen by approximately 4,500 per cent between 1790 and the time of writing. Thus £1 in 1790 is roughly equivalent to £45 today (1996).

CHAPTER ONE

A Small Town in Germany

O NLY A FEW CRUMBLING bricks are left today of the Juden-gasse, a dark, foul-smelling alley in Frankfurt-on-Main where, in the second half of the eighteenth century, a disenfranchised Jew named Meyer Amschel Rothschild founded a European banking dynasty of which it was later said that its history was more important than that of many a royal house.

Rothschild was a man of seemingly inexhaustible energy and ingenuity. His life reflects, as in an old, half-blind mirror, the possibilities as well as the inequities rampant in the Age of Absolutism. He raised five famously gifted sons, veritable money-making machines, to carry on his work after him. Their names overshadowed his own and became synonymous with colossal wealth, extravagant living and hidden political power. A century after his death, the liberal polemicist A. J. Hobson would still ask, in all seriousness, if a great war was still possible in Europe if the House of Rothschild set their face against it. The exaggeration implied in this rhetorical question reflects the odd, and sometimes the lethal way in which the reality of the Rothschilds was subsumed and devoured by the myth.

Until very recently, historians tended to refrain from writing the lives of the underprivileged, especially when they were not politically active or engaged in one of the arts. Such modest men and women were usually dealt with anonymously or quantitatively. Rothschild's origins were certainly modest. There was little reason to foresee his destiny. The personal circumstances of his life were difficult throughout. They suggest a saga not only political and financial but also human and dramatic – more dramatic, perhaps, than that of his flamboyant sons. The sons were not persecuted human beings, legally confined to the squalor of a congested ghetto but, for most of their lives, noblemen, free citizens, living in fairy-tale palaces and socializing with the great of Europe.

The old Judengasse where Rothschild lived his entire life was a narrow lane, more slum-like and overcrowded than any other tenements in Frankfurt. A closed compound, it was shut off from the rest of the city by high walls and three heavy gates. The gates were guarded by soldiers and were locked at night, all day on Sundays and Christian holidays and from Good Friday until after Easter. In it lived the largest Jewish community in Germany in conditions of almost total isolation, or apartheid.

The Judengasse was some ten or twelve feet wide. It ran in a half-circle from the Bornheimer gate in the north to the Jewish cemetery in the south where the oldest tombstones testified to a Jewish presence in the city as far back as the twelfth century. The home of the Rothschild family was a dilapidated tenement, at the back of No 188 Judengasse. Here Meyer Amschel Rothschild was born on 23 February 1744. In 1786, when he had achieved some success, he moved with his wife and children to a larger home at No 148, on the east side of the curving Judengasse, a few doors down from the main synagogue. This was a four story frame-house of brick, wood and slate and, though it was said to be one of the largest in the ghetto, it was so narrow that in the small dark rooms the beds could be placed only along side-walls, at right angles to the street. This house still stood until 18 May 1944, when it was razed – along with much else in central Frankfurt – during an American air-raid.

No trace is left of the house today, nor of the Judengasse itself (except for a few foundation stones), nor of the ancient synagogue, with its high Gothic windows and raised central nave surrounded by carved pews on its four sides, which Rothschild visited almost every day. Frankfurt was badly damaged during the war and was afterwards rebuilt from its ruins and modernized, more radically perhaps, than other German cities. A few well-known buildings in the old city center were reconstructed to appear (on the outside) more or less as they did before, in brand-new Gothic or Baroque. They have since acquired a patina of their own and look almost genuinely old. The most prominent sites were faithfully rebuilt from the ground up – the main churches, the fine burgher's mansion where Goethe was born, five years after Rothschild and a few characteristic old inns. The old town hall was also restored as was the great cathedral, where, until after 1792, the Holy Roman Emperors of the German Nation were crowned. The rest of the city is almost entirely modern. The old street plan was discarded. Where the old Judengasse ran in a wide curve round the old Dominican convent, with its fine altar by Dürer and Holbein, there is now nothing left but a wide expanse of asphalt parking lots and wide avenues choked with traffic and tall office buildings. The Dominican convent was also rebuilt. And by one of those coincidences which, in Germany, are so often pregnant with heavy irony – the remains of the old Judengasse are now buried under the sleek offices of the local gas works.

In Rothschild's day, Frankfurt was a major trade center, as it still is today, a city of merchants, bankers and craftsmen. Bankers often doubled as wholesale merchants, hence the so-called "merchant bankers". There was much need of merchant bankers in Frankfurt. Favored by a unique geographic position, the city was at the junction of five major international land routes linking England and the Netherlands with Russia and Venice and France with the Hanseatic towns of the north. Equally important, at a time when down-river transport was the cheapest and most efficient, was Frankfurt's position on the banks of the river Main, close to where that river flowed into the Rhine, Europe's most important artery.

Long intervals of peace during the first half of the eighteenth century had increased Frankfurt's wealth and population. By mid-century, the city's massive fortifications were crumbling and the old bastions had been planted with trees. Ramparts were converted to public promenades. Frankfurt's population at mid-century was 32,000. Some 3,000 were Jews, locked in a ghetto, subjected to constant humiliations and to punitive levels of taxation. Yet the age was widely known as "enlightened". Montesquieu probably had Frankfurt in mind when, because of its treatment of the Jews, he refused to call his age "enlightened" and instead referred to it as "barbaric".

Though proudly calling itself a Free Imperial City, Frankfurt's inhabitants enjoyed few liberties. Indeed it was a rather despotic

Frankfurt was a "Free" Imperial City. Coronation of Joseph II as Holy Roman
Emperor of the German Nation in Frankfurt Cathedral, 1764; oil painting,
school of Martin von Meytens. (*Courtesy Jewish Museum, Frankfurt.*)

place, being neither as fully independent nor as relatively tolerant as the free Hanseatic city-states of Hamburg and Bremen. In his memoirs, Goethe recorded a public book-burning in Frankfurt he had witnessed in his youth. Voltaire made a brief but ill-advised stop in Frankfurt on his flight from Berlin, only to be summarily thrown into prison at the request of Frederick the Great to make

Local power was in the hands of the privileged and rich; Frankfurt's senior burgomaster Erasmus Schlosser (Cornelia Goethe's father-in-law) and second burgomaster Nikolaus Hupka. Oil painting, Friedrich Ludwig Hauck, 1757. (*Courtesy Deutsches Hochstift, Frankfurt.*)

him surrender letters deemed important to the Prussian King.

The city's supreme sovereign was the emperor, or kaiser, in Vienna, in his capacity as head of the Holy Roman Empire. The "empire" was a loose collection of states and reigning princes who acknowledged the suzerainty of the "emperor". An amorphous, almost pre-historic body, the "empire" claimed its descent from Charlemagne (who built a villa at Frankfurt, not far from the Juden-gasse) and from Julius Caesar (Caesar = kaiser). The empire covered, it was often said with confusion, the territory of present day Austria, Germany, Belgium and the Czech Republic. It comprised 238 political entities headed by ninety-four kings and princes, some at war with one another, 103 counts, forty-one church prelates, and fifty-one Free Imperial Cities, of which Frankfurt was one. At mid-century this ramshackle, incoherent empire was in the final stages of disintegration. It was the butt of almost universal mockery and disdain – but not in Frankfurt: perhaps because it was in Frankfurt that upon the death of a Holy Roman Emperor the new one would be elected in accordance with the elaborate ceremonial laid down in the Golden Bull of 1356.

Local power in the city was in the hands of the privileged and rich, an oligarchy of patrician families and wholesale merchants referred to as "Peppersacks" and "Barrelsquires". All were of the Lutheran faith. Only Lutherans had the right to own land, engage in unrestricted trade or be appointed to the city government – the senate. The senate itself was self-perpetuating and acted as both judiciary and legislature. The correct form in which to address it included no fewer than eleven honorific adjectives. Several hundred Dutch Calvinists and French Huguenots were long settled in Frankfurt but could not publicly worship there. To attend church they had to go "abroad", to the nearby village of Bockenheim in the adjacent landgravate of Hesse. The tax system favored the rich. The maximum taxable fortune was 15,000 gulden.

Jews were by no means newcomers in the city but had lived there for centuries, perhaps since Roman times. They had mostly been traders and craftsmen and the remarkable thing about them was that most Jewish males were, as a rule, literate. They were the only ethnic group that, during the Christianization of Europe, had insisted on its right to remain loyal to its own religion, but at a terrible price. Their "protected" status had gradually deteriorated into a kind of servitude; as so-called "serfs of the Imperial Chamber", they were gradually stripped of most of their rights and reduced to objects, like hay or cattle, which their owner could sell, mortgage, massacre or give away as a gift. Worse than the status of Jews was, perhaps, only that of the wretched, illiterate peasantry, who could be pressed into forced labour or sold as soldiers to fight the wars of foreign potentates. Ludwig I of Bavaria, Holy Roman Emperor from 1314 to 1347, defined the Jews' status thus: "You are Ours in body and possession, We may make, do and deal with you as it pleases Us."

In 1349, Charles IV made use of this right and mortgaged his Frankfurt Jews to the city senate for 15,200 pfund heller (a sum which in 1864 was estimated as the equivalent of US$400,000), thereby reducing them to the serfs of the city. Before the year was out they were made to feel their new legal position during a massacre that wiped out more than half their population. The mortgage was never repaid and, in 1685, Leopold I formally renounced his right to

An early pogrom: the looting of the Judengasse in 1614. Engraving by Matthäus Merian the Elder, 1642. (*Courtesy Jewish Museum, Frankfurt.*)

Ich bitt euch jub leicht mir zů hand/ Was eüch gebürt gebt mir verstand/
Bar gelt auff bürgen oder pfand/

A Jewish moneylender with abacus and peasant client, woodcut, 1531. The text reads: "I ask you Jew, lend me some cash/against security or bail/and tell me what's your due." Note the mock Hebrew letters on the moneylender's coat. (*Courtesy Jewish Museum, Frankfurt.*)

redeem the pledged article. All Jews who henceforth were allowed to settle in Frankfurt automatically came under the control of the senate as its serfs. Tolerated or oppressed, at times massacred, at others only expelled, robbed and tolerated again, they were always at the mercy of the moment, subjected to elaborate rules, enunciated from time to time, known as the *Judenstättigkeit* (Jews' Statute).

In the second half of the eighteenth century, the most recent such Statute, issued in 1616, was still in force. It regulated the personal and professional lives of Frankfurt Jews down to minute details. It severely limited their freedom of occupation and of movement; and it imposed loyalty oaths on Jews which included particularly humiliating references to them as members of an "accursed" race. In a city where Jews were discriminated against by the authorities and habitually massacred by the population, they had to pay an annual tax for the protection of their person and property. Hence the term *Schutzjuden* (literally "protected Jews"). In the Middle Ages they had still been free to reside anywhere in the city; after 1460 they were compelled to live in the overcrowded Judengasse only. Even in the Judengasse, they could not own land, only the houses on it. They were not allowed to farm, trade in weapons, spices and most other commodities. A few rich Jews dealt in luxury goods, jewellery, silk and lace. By 1760, when this story starts, most Frankfurt Jews were pawnbrokers, moneychangers and dealers in second-hand goods.

How they managed to survive under these circumstances and at times even to prosper was a mark of human enterprise and ingenuity. Until 1726 they were required to display on their outer garments the special insignia stipulated in the *Stättigkeit* (for men, two yellow concentric rings, for women a striped veil). After 1726 they were still forbidden to leave the ghetto after dark or on Sundays and during any Christian holiday. The maximum number of Jewish families in Frankfurt was limited to 500. To maintain it below that figure, only twelve Jewish weddings were authorized each year. No couple could marry before the bridegroom reached the age of twenty-five. Frequent house controls (known as "visitations") were conducted by city officials to make sure all these regulations were kept. Jews were often molested in the streets. At the cry "Jud mach mores" – roughly "Jew pay your dues" – they would have to take off their hats, step aside and bow.

On weekdays they had to be in the Judengasse by nightfall, when the gates were locked until the following morning. Some of the more important Jewish tradesmen were at one time somehow able to rent storage space for their wares outside the ghetto in the nearby Fahrgasse, though they had to be careful not to display signs or offer anything for sale there. The senate ordered these closed in 1697. The Jews appealed against this decree at the highest imperial court in Vienna, starting a legal battle which was still undecided in 1806 when the Holy Roman Empire of the German Nation expired.

A vigorous *Kleiderordnung* (Clothes Ordinance) constrained men from wearing berets or anything but "modest" clothing, and women from putting on silk or jewellery (except on Sabbath). Fines for violating these rules ranged from five to twenty thaler. Jews were strictly forbidden to enter the public gardens as they would be 200

A Jewish pawnbroker or moneylender (standing to the left of the group, wearing the obligatory yellow patch and hat) in conversation with Christian noblemen, woodcut, 1731. (*Courtesy Jewish Museum, Frankfurt.*)

years later under the Nazis. They were able to buy vegetables and fruit in the public market only at certain hours, after Christian house-wives had done their shopping. Prison sentences threatened those who dared to watch the procession on Corpus Christi.

No other German city in the eighteenth century imposed such harsh conditions on its Jewish residents. In a city of hard-boiled businessmen the predominant reasons for such measures, as Heine suggested, must have been commercial rivalry: "He was a Frankfurter and so spoke badly of the Jews who had lost all sense of beauty and were selling English goods at 25 per cent under the factory price."

Until the French revolution, Jews were allowed to enter the rest of the city only on business, never for leisure and never more than two abreast. They were forbidden to linger in a public square, visit an inn or coffee house, enter a park or walk in one of the new promenades. They could not hire a Christian servant. They were banned at all times from the vicinity of Frankfurt's main cathedral and could enter the town hall only through a back entrance. Not all of these prohibitions were always enforced and some were observed only sporadically. On the rare occasions when the senate agreed to relax one of the more stringent regulations, self-satisfied and mean-spirited merchants in the town guilds rose up to oppose it. As Heine, the great romantic poet, wrote some years later

> *Malice and stupidity*
> *Like street dogs used to mate.*
> *Their brood can still be recognized*
> *By their sectarian hate.*

Germany in the mid-eighteenth century was a cluster of more than a hundred states ruled by absolute sovereigns. It was not even a geographic concept; there were large German speaking communities on the banks of the Volga and across the Carpathian mountains in what is now Rumania. Germany was a linguistic phenomenon. There was no hint of a national consciousness to unite the speakers of more than a dozen German dialects. A man travelling by stage coach from one city to the next was liable to be stopped for customs several times a day. Every petty principality, including Frankfurt, minted its own currency. The only coins from outside the city that were accepted as payment were those which had the same silver content as the Frankfurt gulden. All others had to be exchanged before a purchase could be made. Constant variations in the exchange rates offered knowledgeable moneychangers ample opportunity to profit, provided they maintained close contacts with well-informed correspondents abroad.

With their far-flung family networks Jews were ideally placed for this role. There were over two hundred moneychangers in Frankfurt, many of them Jews. The local market generated a need for letters of credit, bills of exchange and other paper devices to avoid the inconvenience and danger of sending large amounts of gold and silver coinage abroad. Bills of exchange were promissory notes to pay a certain sum to the bearer on a certain date in the future, usually after a few weeks or months. Before their "due" dates, such bills were often traded at a discount. The discounting of bills yielded good profits and was practised by bankers of all religions. Bankers and moneychangers of all faiths were often also wholesalers in English woollens and cotton, Italian silks, French and German wines, lace, spices, dies and tobacco.

Twice a year, at the great spring and autumn fairs that had been held in Frankfurt since the Middle Ages, the city's population of 32,000 swelled by up to two or three thousand more. Tradesmen from all over Germany and nearby Switzerland and France offered their wares. Others came to buy, noblemen from neighboring towns, burghers, adventurers, wandering scholars and knights, and exotics of all kinds; jugglers, magicians, miracle-doctors, acrobats, actors and artists. During the autumn fair of 1763, eleven-year-old Wolfgang Amadeus Mozart and his little sister Nannerl gave a concert at which the Goethes were present and which had to be repeated three times. The life style of the Goethes in their spacious twenty-room town house, with large garden, in the best part of town, is well documented; it illustrates the sharp contrast between the comforts available to Christian burghers in Frankfurt and the discomforts imposed on the disenfranchised Rothschilds who were of – more or less – the same income group but were confined to cramped quarters in the dark, squalid Judengasse.

Jews were forbidden to open shops outside the Judengasse, and when caught peddling were heavily fined. This rule was suspended during the fairs. On such occasions they might even attend the local opera, as we learn from the report of a disaster in 1754 when, during the performance of an Italian opera, the gallery collapsed and "Jewish

"Death and the Merchant". The *danse macabre* in Matthäus Merian's engraving (1649) is an allegory of the perils of a businessman's life in the seventeenth century. "Life is short and you cannot take your riches with you." (*Courtesy Historical Museum, Frankfurt.*)

31

Alter Römer, the square facing the Frankfurt town hall, 1696. The spring
and autumn fairs attracted tradesmen from all over Germany and from
neighboring Switzerland and France. Engraving, 1696.
(*Courtesy Historical Museum, Frankfurt.*)

ladies and Christian gentlemen fell upon each other". The Jews'
contribution to the success of the Frankfurt fairs must have been
considerable. Heine, taken by his father to the Frankfurt fair, was
led through the hustling and pushing and shown "the Jewish as well
as the Christian stands where one is cheated even though one buys
goods at ten percent below the factory price". Heine also visited the
town hall, where the Holy Roman Emperors were elected and where,
as he mocked, emperors were also "bought at ten percent below
factory price. In the end they completely ran out of this commodity."

The main access routes into the city were from the south, over a
many-arched bridge on the river Main. The traveller entering the
city over this bridge saw a busy river port teeming with bearers and
beasts of burden and goods from all corners of the earth. Barrels of
wine, logs of wood and bales of cloth were piled high on the wharves.
Heavily laden boats were pulled upstream by oxen on the shore.

Behind the forest of masts rose a silhouette of battlements and spires, not, perhaps, as majestic as that of Cologne or Mainz but massive enough to be impressive.

On the city-side of the river, the first thing a traveller fell upon was the notorious *Judensau* (Jews' Sow), an obscene painted relief on the wall of the south bridgehead. It was put there and maintained, as Goethe noted, not by some bigoted individual but by the city government. This was significant, he felt. The caricature depicted a fat sow holding up its tail for a Jew, with his tongue hanging out, to lick its excrement. Several other Jews, dressed in the obligatory round and pointed Jews' hats, were shown sucking the sow's teats, while the whole scene was watched over approvingly by a devil.

Behind the bridgehead, one reached the *Fahrtor*, the main harbor gate into the city. Here the post-coaches deposited their passengers. Travellers had to state their provenance and were made to pay a toll. The rate for Christians was four kreuzer; for Jews and oxen led to the market, eight. As he was paying the toll at the *Fahrtor* in 1775,

The notorious *Judensau* (Jews' sow) on the main city gate, put there by the senate. "Drink it, Jew, drink its milk/rabbi, eat its excrement." Anonymous woodcut, *c.* 1470. (Reproduced in Georg Liebe, *Das Judentum in der Deutschen Vergangenheit*, 1903.)

33

Moses Mendelssohn, the philosopher of the enlightenment whom contemporaries were calling "the German Socrates", was asked by a guard: "Jew, what are you selling? I may want to buy something from you." "You'll never want to buy any of my things", Mendelssohn replied. "Well, tell us what you deal in?" insisted the guard. "In reason!", Mendelssohn answered. (Heine said of Mendelssohn, a hunchback, that providence had given him a hump the better to bear his Jewishness.)

On the Fahrgasse, packhorses and heavy wagons harnessed to four or six animals carted goods over cobblestones to and from the wharves. The road was wide enough to allow the heaviest carts to pass. It was lined with shops and stables and workshops with shooing and carpenters' tools outside. To the left, it was only a short walk to the nearby town hall. In open street markets farmers from the nearby countryside offered their wares. The air was saturated with their calls. And everywhere in the crowded streets there was the pungent smell of wood fires, even in summer, for food had to be cooked. Food in Frankfurt was hearty. Fat sausages, cabbages and potatoes were washed down with a local apple wine. Eighteenth-century writers described Frankfurters as lively people, always in a hurry, minding their businesses, speaking a very particular local dialect. Frankfurters were known as "prosaic" people. Ostentation in housing and clothing was frowned upon. The local oligarchy was not headed by a prince with ambitious building projects, but by down-to-earth businessmen who concluded big money transactions in the privacy of their counting houses (*comptoirs*) and tended to understatement in public. The Gothic town hall was plain enough with its unadorned stepped gable. The cathedral was squat and far simpler in decor than those of Nuremberg or Cologne. The merchant-princes lived in large but otherwise plain frame houses. The princes who gathered periodically to elect a new Holy Roman Emperor, and the emperors themselves, were housed in hotels; their large entourages were billeted with burghers. The spirit of the place was workaday and businesslike. Schiller, sending Goethe his poem *Die Teilung der Erde*, an elegy on the vanity of earthly pleasure, wrote that it be best read in Frankfurt, a city ruled "by the God of this world – Money". Goethe wrote back saying that the people of Frankfurt lived in "a frenzy of making money and spending it". In *Faust*, he drew a picture of Mephistopheles' favorite city, clearly a portrait of Frankfurt in the second half of the eighteenth century.

> *I'd choose a typical metropolis*
> *At center, bourgeois stomach's gruesome bliss*
> *Tight crooked alleys, pointed gables, mullions*
> *Crabbed market stalls of roots and scallions*
> *Where bleeding joints on benches lie*
> *Prey to the browsing carrion-fly;*
> *For there at any time you'll find*
> *Ado and stench of every kind.*
> *Then, boulevards and spacious squares*
> *To flaunt aristocratic airs.*
> *And on, past any gates resistance*
> *The suburbs sprawl into the distance.*

Turning right from the Fahrgasse into a quarter thick with stables and storehouses, one quickly reached the northern end of the Judengasse. The Judengasse was sunless for most of the day, a narrow, rank-smelling space. Few Christians entered it. Some merely peered in. In the pale and pasty complexion of its Jews they would see proof of divine guilt and just punishment for the denial and murder, long ago, of Jesus Christ. The young Goethe shared some of these prejudices. In the back of his mind, he confessed in his memoirs, were "the cruelties committed by Jews [*sic*] against Christian children". Throughout his life, Goethe remained preoccupied with the state of the "ominous Judengasse":

The confinement, the dirt, the swarm of people, the accents of an unpleasant tongue, all made a disagreeable impression, even when one only looked in when passing outside the gate. It took a long time before I ventured in alone; and I did not return easily after once escaping the obtrusiveness of so many people untiringly intent on haggling, either demanding or offering . . . And yet, they were also human beings, energetic, agreeable, and even their obstinacy in sticking to their own customs, one could not deny it respect. Moreover, their girls were pretty . . .

The east side of the Judengasse, close to Rothschild's last home. This photograph was taken around 1860. Originally the street was much darker. By 1860 the right-hand side of the street had already been torn down. (*Courtesy Jewish Museum, Frankfurt.*)

The population of the ghetto was by then nearly double that of 200 years earlier. Yet the city refused to allocate ground to enlarge it. Congestion was greater than anywhere else in the city, and getting worse every year. The growing demand for living and working space caused the price of houses in the Judengasse to rise far above that in

Houses at the back of the Judengasse. Note the high wall surrounding
the ghetto. Aquarell by C. T. Reiffenstein, 1857.
(*Courtesy Historical Museum, Frankfurt.*)

the best parts of Frankfurt. (In 1740, a squalid airless four room
house at the northern end of the Judengasse sold for 6,000 gulden,
approximately the same price Goethe's father paid for his fine

burgher's mansion of twenty rooms and garden in the upper-middle class Grosse Hirschgraben.) Since Jews could obtain legal residence in the city only if they owned property in the Judengasse, most of the houses that had originally been built for one family were now shared by two, three or even five families. The parties often took turns in occupying different parts of a house so that each family was able to enjoy the best, airiest rooms once in every five or ten years.

To provide for the growing population, most of the old houses had been subdivided over the years. Two or three protruding floors had been added above. The new floors overhung the narrow street and seemed almost to touch those on the opposite side. To provide even more living space, a second row of houses was built in the narrow backyards, squeezed in between the first row of houses in

Ansicht der Judengasse in Franckfurt am Main, nach dem Brandt.
1. *Eingang der Judengas.* 2. *Synagoge.* 3. *die Judenmauer.* 4. *das neue Brauhaus.* 5. *die Windmühl.*
6. *Kramläden.*

It might be said of the Judengasse what Turgenev said of old Russia: "Our towns burn down every ten or fifteen years." The northern end of the Judengasse after the fire of 1796, the fifth great fire during the eighteenth century. Note the armed guard at the gate (1) and the total destruction between the gate (1) and the synagogue (2). Rothschild's *Hinterpfann* (3) also burnt down. Contemporary copper engraving. (*Courtesy Historical Museum, Frankfurt.*)

Rag dealers in the Judengasse. Idealized oil painting by Carl Schlosser, 1860.
(*Courtesy Jewish Museum, Frankfurt.*)

the Judengasse and the high ghetto walls beyond. Scarcely enough space was left to admit daylight to either.

The northern end of the Judengasse was its most dilapidated – in the words of a traveller in 1747, "somber, humid and filthy". Barely ten feet wide, wagons could not turn around in it. Outside stairs narrowed this part of the street even more. The general gloominess was further enhanced by grim fire walls between the crumbling tenements reaching high above the gables. Parts of the street were unpaved. The air was foul from the sewer that ran through in open, shallow ditches. The anonymous author of a *Travelogue through*

Thuringia (1796) wrote that it was not necessary to ask for directions to the Judengasse, since one could easily smell it from a distance.

The houses were mostly wood, which was cheap, insulated one from the cold and grew nearby. But in a fire, everything burned down – sometimes the entire street. It might have been said of the Judengasse what Turgenev said about old Russia: "Our towns burn down every ten or fifteen years". During the eighteenth century alone, five fires (1711, 1719, 1721, 1774 and 1796) completely wiped out all, or large, parts of the Judengasse, leaving between one third and the entire population destitute.

The language of the ghetto was not Yiddish (which includes many Slavic words), as is often thought, but *Judendeutsch*, a mixture of Hebrew and Frankfurt dialect that was written from right to left in Hebrew letters. German suffixes were added to Hebrew verbs to produce the *Judendeutsch* infinitive. Among non-Jews, *Judendeutsch* was derided as impudent *Mauscheln* (whining). And yet according to Heine, *Mauscheln* was "nothing but the proper language of Frankfurt and is spoken with equal excellence by the circumcised as well as by the non-circumcised population there".

There were four synagogues in the Judengasse, a public bath, a clinic and a communal bakery, where bread was baked on weekdays; for Sabbath they would produce the traditional dish *sholet* (or *cholent*, from the French *chaud-lent*), a hearty cassoulet made of meats and vegetables which Heine celebrated in the "Hebrew Melodies":

> *Sholet lovely spark of heaven*
> *Daughter of Elysium*
> *Thus would sound the Ode of Schiller*
> *Had he ever tasted Sholet.*
> *Sholet is the dish of heaven*
> *Whose immortal recipe*
> *God himself once gave to Moses*
> *Long ago upon Mount Sinai*

But for the consolations of the Sabbath, the endless restrictions imposed from outside may have been unbearable. The Sabbath was entirely consecrated to the synagogue, to learning, to the family and to offering hospitality to strangers. Holidays were celebrated raucously and with gusto.

In one of these tenements, in the back row of the northern Judengasse, Rothschild grew up in a house called *Hinterpfann* (literally "House in the Back of the Saucepan"). As if to compensate for the general gloom, houses in the ghetto often had picturesque, colorful names: Red Shield, White Tulip, Tower, Golden Well, Crown of Roses, Saucepan, Elephant, Ship, Green Jar. Although their civil status was often uncertain, the inhabitants of the Judengasse, like

Houses at the back of the Judengasse behind the remains of the high ghetto wall (*c.* 1840) which resemble how Rothschild's *Hinterpfann* must have looked. In his day, windows had to be boarded up to prevent Jews from looking into the Christian city on the right. Drawing by Peter Becker, 1872. (*Courtesy Jewish Museum, Frankfurt.*)

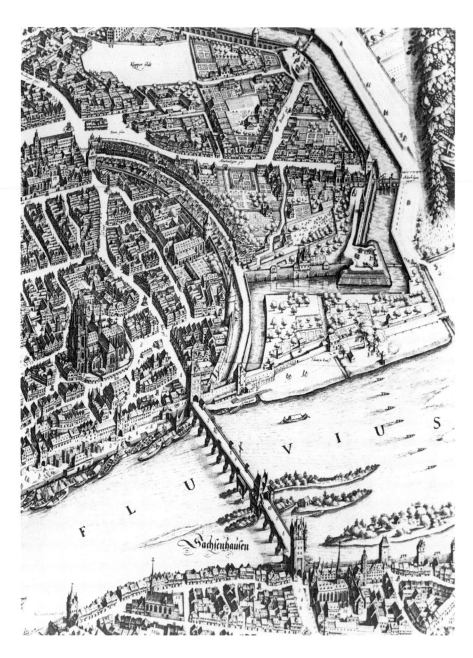

A plan of Frankfurt showing the bridge across the river Main, the main
entrance to the Fahrgasse. To the left, the cathedral; to the right, the arching
Judengasse behind the ghetto wall. The *Hinterpfann* was a tenement in the
back of a house on the Judengasse at its northern (upper) end.
The Rothschilds moved there in 1664. Engraving by Matthäus
Merian the Elder, 1628. (*Courtesy Historical Museum, Frankfurt.*)

aristocrats in rags, derived a proud sense of identity from their squalid ancestral homes. Many took their surnames from their houses. Pictorial representations of these names, like coats of arms, were engraved, painted or embroidered on keystones and doors, household utensils, rings, book bindings, scarves, handkerchiefs and tombstones. People retained their names – and emblems – when they moved to another house.

This happened to the Rothschilds. The name has been traced back to Isaak Elchanan Rothschild, who derived his appellation from a small house he occupied at the southern end of the Judengasse called *zum Roten Schild* (at the Red Shield). In 1577, according to the public record, Isaak Elchanan Rothschild paid an annual tithe on his assets amounting 2,700 gulden. When his grandson Naftali Hirz left the house at the Red Shield in 1664 and moved to the *Hinterpfann*, he took the name Rothschild with him.

Of Naftali Hirz and Rothschild's other forefathers we know little more than their names and the general modesty of their circumstances. Early in the eighteenth century there were ten or twelve Rothschilds in Frankfurt, changing money or buying and selling cloth (or second-hand goods). Sons of the Rothschild family were often given their fathers' first name as their middle name. The eighteenth-century *Memorbuch* – death register – of the Jewish community of Frankfurt lists the names and main attributes of the better-known residents of the Judengasse and acclaims several of these Rothschilds for their honesty, piety and concern for the welfare of the poor. Rothschild's great-grandfather Kalman died in 1707; four years before his death he was assessed at 6,000 gulden for which he would have paid an annual tax of at least 200. He is said to have dealt in silk and wool cloth, though probably not very heavily, as trade in silk was still forbidden to Jews under the law. His main business was moneychanging, as was that of his son, Rothschild's grandfather, Moses Kalman (also called Bauer) who traded in crepe and died on 19 October 1735. During his lifetime the *Hinterpfann* burned down twice, in the fires of 1711 and 1719. He paid an annual tax of only eight gulden. These figures do not necessarily indicate the real extent of his assets but they reflect the ups and downs within the ghetto's middle and lower-middle class.

The bridge across the river Main in 1742, looking west. The *Fahrtor* is on the right. Note the cathedral towers next to it. The ghetto was on the extreme right. Drawing by C. G. Schultz (*Courtesy Historical Museum, Frankfurt.*)

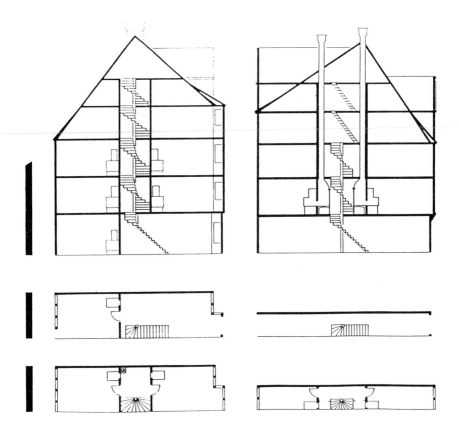

A cross section through the four front and back houses at the northern end of the Judengasse that shows who lived there according to the censuses of 1703 and 1709. The Rothschild's *Hinterpfann* could have been the back house on the extreme left. In it lived four families comprising twenty-seven people in an area of approximately 1000 square feet. In the front house lived two families,

Grandfather Moses Kalman is said to have had business dealings with Josef Suss Oppenheimer (Jud Suss), the notorious protagonist of many antisemitic diatribes. Oppenheimer was the privileged director of finances for the Duke of Württemberg. In his prime as a Court-Jew, Oppenheimer had been able to live in Frankfurt with his mistresses outside of the ghetto, at the elegant Hotel zum Goldenen Schwan where visiting foreign potentates also stayed. A vain, power-hungry man, he made many enemies. After the Duke's death, he was tortured and hanged publicly in a cage.

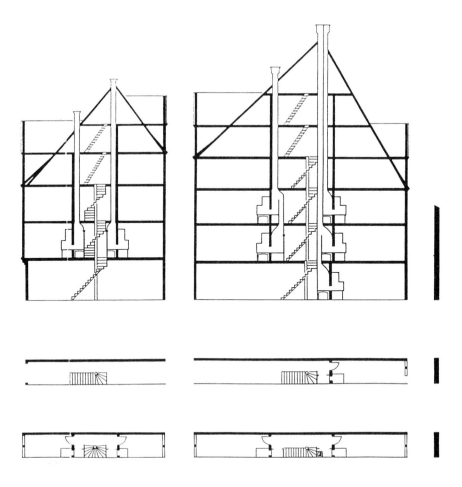

a total of nine people. On the west side of the Judengasse, the front house contained four families, a total of twenty-eight people. The house at the back of it contained two families, or fourteen people. Chart drawn to scale.
(*Courtesy Jewish Museum, Frankfurt.*)

The lesson of Oppenheimer's execution was not lost on his Jewish contemporaries. It taught them to hide their wealth, if they had any, and not be tempted by the pursuit of power. The majority remained poor. Rothschild's father, Amschel Moses, was a modest money-changer who also traded in silk cloth. The *Memorbuch* lauds his "charity" and the "hospitality" of his home. His declared assets in 1749, a total of 1375 gulden, reflected his position in the Judengasse at the very bottom of the lower-middle class.

Amschel Moses Rothschild and his wife Schöenche had eight

children. Five survived the disastrous sanitary conditions in the Jud-engasse. Meyer Amschel Rothschild was the fourth child. Little exposed to the sun, the *Hinterpfann* was damp and chilly in winter, humid and fly-infested in summer. It was reached from the street by a narrow corridor through the house in front. The cramped yard between the two houses was often muddy or flooded with waste waters that would not run off. Outline plans of the houses on the Judengasse still exist in the Frankfurt city archive. They give an idea of *Hinterpfann's* dimensions and position in the back of the street. Less than ten feet wide, its total area (on three floors and an attic) was roughly nine hundred square feet. The house was shared by two families (the other family was named Bauer), a total, presumably, of ten or twelve people. It accommodated their businesses as well.

On the ground floor one entered a dim office where accounts and bales of cotton and silk cloth, a main source of income for both families, were kept. The only light came from an opening above the door. The windowless, steep stairway had no balustrade; one pulled oneself up holding on to braided ropes, which were said to have been a cause of skin infections and scabs. Wood was stored in a small cellar. Kitchens and living rooms were upstairs. The five Rothschild children shared a small bedroom. Clothes and linens were kept in wooden boxes and barrels. Every corner, every nook up to the roof was used. The attic was reached by a loose ladder, which could be pulled up to protect the residents from a rioting mob, and its small windows were boarded up. This was in compliance with a municipal ordinance which forbade Jews to look into Christian houses and gardens on the other side of the ghetto wall.

Young Meyer Amschel Rothschild received a traditional Jewish education. This had hardly changed since the early Middle Ages. Its aim was to impart complete devotion to God, knowledge of the Torah and Talmud and strict observance of all the commandments. A steady ritual of learning and prayer accompanied him from an early age. Soon after his birth, according to ancient custom, a *minyan*, ten men, relatives and neighbors, would have gathered around him at the *Hinterpfann*. After placing a copy of the Pentateuch in his cradle, they would pronounce: "May this boy observe what is written in this book." Early every morning and in the evening at sunset the

The synagogue in the Judengasse. Aquarrell by C. T. Reiffenstein *c.* 1854.
(*Courtesy Jewish Museum, Frankfurt.*)

Schul-Klopper (synagogue-herald) walked up and down the Juden-gasse knocking on every door with his hammer summoning his father, and the other men in the Judengasse, to prayer. On the Sabbath, when hammering was forbidden, the *Schul-Klopper* pounded on doors with his fist which he protected with a piece of cloth to avoid bruising.

49

The *heder* (schoolroom) behind the synagogue. The Judengasse was a
center of Jewish learning. Aquarell by C. T. Reiffenstein, 1865–70.
(*Courtesy Jewish Museum, Frankfurt.*)

As soon as Rothschild could walk he would rise each morning
with the *Schul-Klopper* and accompany his father to the synagogue
where low benches were provided for children close to the high
wooden pews. On Sabbath eve, as soon as prayers were over, he
would run home to alert his mother and find that she had already lit
the traditional Sabbath candles. As the child grew, he heard so many
prayers and benedictions repeated so often he knew some of them
by heart before he was three or four when, like other little boys, he
was sent with a slate and a bit of chalk to a *heder*.

The word means simply "room". It originated at a time when a
special room in or near a synagogue was set aside for teaching the
young. There were several *heders* in the Judengasse. In all matters of
education the ghetto was self-governing. Education was obligatory
for all boys up to the age of thirteen. (It was not yet obligatory in
the rest of Frankfurt, where the rate of school attendance at that
time is thought to have been less than 60 per cent.) There were
almost twice as many teachers per pupil in the ghetto than in the

rest of the city. The Frankfurt Judengasse was a center of Jewish learning. Students from near and far flocked to its *yeshiva* (Talmud academy) led by luminaries known all over the Jewish European world. Rothschild's *heder* was in the school house behind the old synagogue. The atmosphere of learning in this school house was enhanced by the presence there, *in clausura*, of several renowned Talmud scholars, the so-called *Claus*. At mid-century the community boasted eight rabbis, twelve teachers, five cantors, one notary and two doctors. Distant Jewish communities recognized its importance and consulted its rabbis on matters of Jewish law.

There was, of course, a pervasive addiction to money and trade in the Judengasse, but for learners and scholars of all ages it was saturated at the same time with a uniquely motivating atmosphere. In the Judengasse the learned enjoyed a unique prestige, on a par

Despite a pervasive addiction to money and trade in the Judengasse, for potential scholars of all ages it was saturated with a uniquely motivating atmosphere. Schoolboy in the Judengasse. Oil painting by J. A. B. Nothnagel, date unknown. (*Courtesy Jewish Museum, Frankfurt.*)

with, if not higher than, that of the few rich. It was a peculiarity of Jewish ghetto life at the time that the richest, most successful merchants, jewellers or moneychangers, were sometimes also the most learned Talmudic scholars.

The education provided by the *heder* was entirely religious. All forms of knowledge outside the sacred books were ignored. Instruction centered on the Torah and its interpretations to the exclusion of everything else. Instruction was by rote. The Hebrew alphabet was taught first. The children learned how to combine letters into words and words into verses in holy scripture. Classes in the *heder* began early in the morning and lasted through most of the day. Instruction for all age groups was conducted simultaneously in the same room, although in a large community like Frankfurt, the teacher would have had an assistant, a *behelfer*. While the head teacher taught the three to five-year olds, the older children, supervised by the assistant, would be repeating their own lessons.

The five books of Moses were read through systematically, verse after verse – first in Hebrew, then translated into *Judendeutsch*. Every verse was elucidated in the light of Rashi's commentaries which for centuries had enlightened Jewish school children and fascinated their elders. The teacher ruled with an iron hand, freely using the cane. The children soon knew large portions of the Pentateuch by heart, beginning with Genesis and its listing of divine utterances by which the world had been created – "And God said: Let there be light" – to the death of Moses at the end of Deuteronomy.

The languages of instruction were *Judendeutsch* and Hebrew. Rothschild must have been more or less fluent in both by the time he was six. Neither language was taught as such but imparted. There was no instruction in grammar and none in the Bible beyond the five books of Moses. As soon as that stage was reached, by which time Rothschild was seven or eight, he began to tackle the elaborate exegesis of the Talmud and the even more elaborate exegesis-of-the-exegesis. The Talmud added a third language, Aramaic, to the curriculum.

Its main purpose was to impart a thorough knowledge of Jewish Law; the emphasis was on explication and elucidation, a never-ending exercise in memory and concentration, a course in logic and systematic thought. Whatever else this education achieved – or failed to achieve within its overly narrow horizons – it was said to sharpen the mind like no other and imbue pupils with an intellect quicker and more agile than that of the average graduate of a German high school.

But if, in the sixteenth century, Jewish men had still been thought to be among the best educated in Germany, by the eighteenth, the gap between traditional education and the surrounding culture had widened so much that a purely Jewish education was widely regarded as insufficient. There were no secular studies whatsoever at the *heder*, and the German language was ignored. It is a mystery how, leaving school at thirteen with no instruction in arithmetic, or in reading and writing German, Jewish boys afterwards coped with real life in the business world. Rothschild may have had private tutors who taught him German and some arithmetic and geography at home, but this is uncertain and, on the whole, quite improbable. In later years he would write *Judendeutsch* in a beautiful Hebrew hand. His handwriting in German was adequate but his vocabulary remained limited, his syntax awkward and his spelling erratic throughout his life.

At home, from an early age, he was apprenticed in the family business. Everybody in the family, boys and girls, were expected to help. Rothschild was sent out on errands to other moneychangers in the street. During the great autumn fair, when business was especially brisk, the boy helped his father sort out the coins he had exchanged for local money. Ducats, louis d'ors, carolins, gulden and thaler of all sorts passed through his hands and occasionally coins and medals of some rare or historical value, which elicited an early interest in numismatics.

In the *Hinterpfann* and in the long, monotonous routine of the *heder*, he passed a joyless childhood, a pale, slim boy never able to play in a park or leave the sunless street, except in an emergency. Along the entire length of the Judengasse there was not a single tree, nor a bush or another patch of green.

Early in 1755, when the boy had just passed his eleventh birthday, his father took him out of school and sent him to Fürth, a small town outside Nuremberg in Bavaria, to complete his education in the

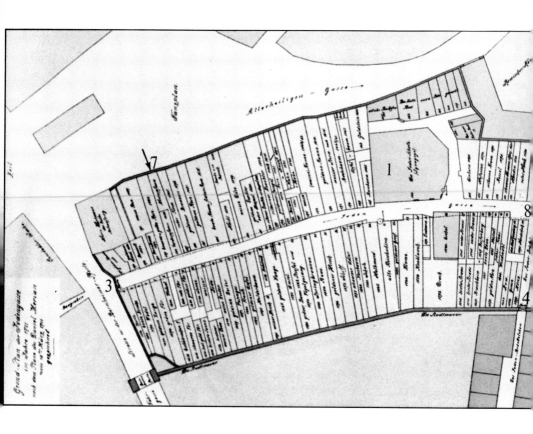

Plan of the Judengasse by Daniel Merian, 1711. The *Hinterpfann* is in the
back row on the left (northern) end of the Judengasse, fifth house.
(Original lost. Reproduced in Alexander Dietz, *Stammbuch der Frankfurter
Juden*, Frankfurt 1907.)

Jewish seminary. The journey took three days by stage-coach. The
reasons for this move can no longer be ascertained. The Jewish
seminary of Fürth was a well-known training ground for rabbis and
his father may have intended him to become one, though this is
unlikely: it would have been easier and cheaper to attend the
rabbinical seminary in Frankfurt. Rothschild's instruction at Fürth
continued what he had begun in the Frankfurt *heder*. It consisted of
intensive courses in Talmudic law. Ethical questions were explored
through the elucidation of sacred texts. There may have been some
instruction in secular subjects such as arithmetic but again this is
uncertain.

A few months after the boy's departure from Frankfurt an epi-
demic of smallpox swept through the disease-infested Judengasse.

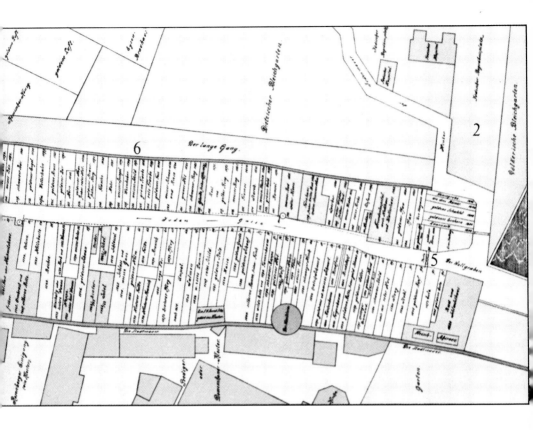

1 Synagogue; 2 Cemetery; 3 North Gate; 4 Center Gate;
5 South Gate; 6 Back Ghetto Wall; 7 *Hinterpfann*; 8 "Green Shield".

Rothschild's father Amschel Moses died on 6 October 1755; the boy was not yet twelve-years old. His mother Schöenche died nine months later, on 29 June 1756. In the meantime, the Seven Years' War had broken out and the roads had become unsafe. But soon after his mother's death, Rothschild must have left Fürth and returned to Frankfurt. With his sisters Belche and Gutelche, and his brothers Kalman Amschel and Moses Amschel, he was now in the care of relatives. They had jointly inherited the *Hinterpfann*. Each had come into a few hundred gulden in cash, payable upon their reaching maturity. Rothschild's older brother could be of only little help to him. As a thirteen-year-old orphan, with a few coins in his pocket, the future tycoon launched out alone into the world.

Family connections had secured him an apprenticeship at the

banking firm of Wolf Jakob Oppenheim in Hanover. The choice of firm revealed foresight, ambition and design. The Oppenheims were a prominent family of bankers which in the past one-hundred years had branched out from the Frankfurt Judengasse to Vienna, Stuttgart, Bonn, Hildesheim and Hanover. At their branch in Hanover, young Rothschild could acquire experience in finance and learn the fine art of being a Court-Jew – the only career in the Age of Absolutism that enabled a Jew to escape the limitations and humiliations imposed on him by the law.

Every ambitious Jewish merchant at the time must have aspired to become a Court-Jew. The Oppenheims were a family of Court-Jews or court-agents well-known throughout Europe. Wolf Jakob Oppenheim's grandfather, Samuel Oppenheim, had been Court-Factor to the Austrian Emperor, helping him finance his wars against the Turks and against Louis XIV. His uncle was court-agent to the Prince-Bishop Clemens August of Cologne.

Court-Jews were a peculiarly German phenomenon, especially in the smaller principalities that competed with one another in the pursuit of luxuries. Princes were in constant need of credit to furnish their armies with guns, their mistresses with jewellery, their courtiers with fine cloth and their cooks with French and Italian delicacies. Nowhere in Europe were there so many Court-Jews as in Germany. There was little call for them in France, where the central bureaucracy was more developed, or in Italy, where an advanced banking system had existed since the late Middle Ages. In the relatively backward German lands, Court-Jews – products of "absolutism, mercantilism and baroque culture" – used their family contacts across Europe to supply kings and princes with the credit they needed to pay for their personal and political extravagances.

A story was told of a certain Jew who, upon being asked why Jews were so proud though they had no princes and no part in any government, replied haughtily, "We are not princes yet we govern them". Court-Jews, perhaps because of their isolation from both Jewish and Christian society, tended to intermarry. By the eighteenth century their marriages in many ways resembled the internationally-inclined marriage habits of the aristocracy.

Mostly because princes made their own laws and were known to renege on contracts, Christian bankers were often reluctant to be court-agents. Jews had fewer choices and were more willing to risk a court-agent's uncertain fate. Not all Court-Jews, of course, were always at risk. There were intimate relationships occasionally between a sovereign and his Jew, though these were rare. Count Lippe-Detmold wrote charmingly to his banker Joseph Isaac in about 1735: "Joseph, we have no butter for this evening, so I am asking you to make arrangements to have a full barrel here tonight. There is no time to lose, otherwise we can't sit down at table, so I hope you'll do your best."

The Hanover house of Oppenheim, to which Rothschild was sent at some point in 1757, was a small merchant bank with princely clients in Holland and northern Germany. Rothschild may have been happier in Hanover than he had been in Frankfurt or Fürth. Instead of the deadly monotony of study there was the lively traffic of a small bank. Hanover belonged to the English crown, and consequently the atmosphere there was more liberal and relaxed. Nearby Göttingen was the most liberal university in Germany. Jews were disenfranchised in Hanover as they were in Frankfurt, but they were not molested by street urchins during the day nor locked into a ghetto at night.

There is no record that Rothschild returned to Frankfurt during the next seven years. (In the course of the Seven Years' War, Frankfurt was occupied by French troops and from 1759 to 1763 it was administered by a French military governor.) In Hanover Rothschild gained experience in foreign trade, and learned how to issue or cash bills of exchange. His own functions at the bank were lowly enough, especially during the first three or four years. Apprenticeship in the eighteenth century was a form of bondage. Apprentices were bound to their employers for predetermined periods of service. The first two or three years were often spent in menial work, serving the master and his family as a porter and general factotum. Apprentices were paid no salaries but received free board and lodgings, usually in the master's house. Besides learning the rudiments of the financial business, Rothschild broadened his knowledge of rare and antique coins and historic medals. Coins had fascinated him since early childhood. The Oppenheim bank had a rare coin department and his work there gave him an opportunity to deepen his expertise. His general education still left a good deal to be desired. But he was acquiring a certain amount of historical knowledge without which he might not have been able to find his way in numismatics with only a religious training. Coins and medals – Roman, Persian, Byzantine or more modern – attracted collectors who often bought them as an investment. Rothschild met them across the counter at the Hanover bank. He must have done a little business in old coins on his own. By the time he was eighteen, he had become something of an expert. A scientific numismatic catalogue, the first of its kind, had just been published and Rothschild acquired it. He read every other book or paper he could find on the subject. And he happened to encounter a young Hanoverian nobleman, a General von Estorff, who was an ardent coin collector and took a liking to him. Estorff commissioned Rothschild to locate and buy for him certain coins and medals for his collection. It was an acquaintance that would prove useful to Rothschild later on.

CHAPTER TWO

First Steps

In 1763, THE PEACE of Hubertusburg finally ended the Seven Years' War and the French occupation of Frankfurt. A few months later, Rothschild returned to his home town, bringing his Hanover savings with him. Unlike his father and his grandfather before him, he had learned to observe the affairs of the world from another vantage point than the Judengasse. Hanover was more liberal than Frankfurt and he might have wanted to stay there. But as an outsider, he had no recognized civil status in the city. With the end of his apprenticeship at the Oppenheim bank, his residence permit in Hanover would end too.

Hanover may also have seemed too small to the ambitious young man. Frankfurt, not Hanover, was the leading German commercial center. His brothers and sisters were in Frankfurt and the rest of his family, and he had inherited one quarter of his parents' old house, the *Hinterpfann*, at the rear of the Judengasse. In Frankfurt he was a kind of second- or third-class citizen. However unsatisfactory or degrading, he had a kind of status there, without which, at mid-century, a Jew had no rights whatsoever and was almost an outlaw.

Frankfurt had changed in the years since his departure. The French military occupation had caused discomfort and loss as well as improvements. The military governor, Thoranc, billeted in Goethe's parents' house, introduced house numbers and street lights, although residents who went out at night were still obliged to carry lanterns, as in the old days, stratified according to their civic status: the number of lit candles allowed inside each lantern reflected a man's rank – three for noblemen, two for burghers, one for servants and Jews with permits to leave the Judengasse after dark. Because of its extreme congestion the Judengasse had been spared the billeting of French

A rag shop in the Judengasse. Aquarell by C. T. Reiffenstein, 1852.
(*Courtesy Historical Museum, Frankfurt.*)

troops which had made life uncomfortable in other parts of the city. But trade also suffered under the French. The money business was in trouble because of the proliferation during the war, as a deliberate Prussian strategy, of coins with reduced silver content. The economy was in stagnation.

Under these inauspicious circumstances, Rothschild moved back into the *Hinterpfann*. His older brother, Moses, was now married and lived there with his family, his younger invalid brother, Calmann, and a couple of other relatives. The three brothers owned only three quarters of the house; like so many other houses in the ghetto, the remaining quarter was owned by these relatives. Moses and Calmann had their businesses downstairs. Moses ran a pawnbroker's shop and traded in second-hand goods. Pawnbroking in Frankfurt was often a form of storage business. It enabled traders from outside attending the fair to deposit unsold surpluses against payment until the next fair. The youngest brother, Calmann, was a moneychanger.

Rothschild's share of his late father's estate could not have amounted to more than a few hundred gulden. With this capital he joined Calmann's exchange shop as a partner and added the business to which he had been apprenticed in Hanover – trade in rare coins, medals and other curios, quaint jewels, engravings and antiques. The brothers' pursuits were radically different. The confusion on the ground floor and in the cellar must have been considerable.

Living conditions in the house, and life generally for the Jews of Frankfurt, had scarcely improved in the seven years since Rothschild had left. The *Hinterpfann* was only a few steps from the northern gate to the Judengasse into which Goethe, and many others, had peered with so much morbid fascination or disgust. In Hanover, Rothschild had been spared some of the restrictions and humiliations that marked daily life in the Judengasse. The first time the heavy wooden doors on the northern gate slammed shut behind him, shortly after sunset, must have come as a shock – he had experienced nothing like it in Hanover. By order of the senate the gates now closed not only at night and on Sundays and holidays but also on Friday mornings until after mass. In the case of an emergency, if a midwife had to be called or medicines fetched from the pharmacy, Jews had to walk as quickly as they could and take the shortest route through the Christian town or "suffer a fine". When, a short time after Rothschild's return, the city was swept by the pomp of another imperial coronation, Jews were again locked into their quarter for the duration, even though they were also constrained to present precious gifts of cash and jewellery to the imperial couple and their entourage.

Most Christians still addressed Jews harshly, and in the familiar second person *Du*, as they did servants or serfs. Jews caught walking more than two abreast in the Christian town paid a fine of fifty kreuzer. Those with no cash on them had their hats confiscated by the guards as security against payment. The self-image of the city was changing, however, a fact reflected in the Frankfurt City Calendars. This richly illustrated semi-official publication no longer highlighted the city's martial character, its massive walls and battlements,

The new parks planted on the old ramparts. Until 1806 Frankfurt was the
only city in Europe where Jews were banned from public parks, as they would
be a century later under the Nazis. Pencil drawing by T. F. Beer, 1794.
(*Courtesy Historical Museum, Frankfurt.*)

as in the past. The views now shown were more pastoral than before
the Seven Years' War. The emphasis was on trade and the river
Main. The only human figure shown was that of a man, deeply
immersed in a book, emerging from one of the city gates to wander
in the idyllic landscape surrounding it. The old ramparts were now
all planted with trees and turned into promenades, though the sign
outside one of the promenades said:

> *Kein Jud und kein Schwein*
> *Darf hier hinein.*
> *[No Jew or pig can enter here]*

The growing congestion in the Judengasse made the quest for fresh
air by those living there more urgent than ever before. Spokesmen
for the community addressed the "most noble and illustrious city
council", complaining that there was:

no other place in Germany where Jews are so restricted in
the enjoyment of fresh air and of a clean street as we are . . .
Jews in Vienna enter public promenades without hindrance.
In Mainz and Mannheim and in [nearby] Hanau the parks
are open [to Jews] . . . only we are denied [this right].

The authorities dismissed this appeal as one more proof "of the
boundless arrogance of this nation which makes every effort at every
opportunity to achieve equality". The consequences of granting such
a request could be disastrous, the authorities claimed: women walking
on the promenade might be "harassed" by the arrival of "hordes
of Jews".

Rothschild was now in his early twenties, a tall young man, with large
penetrating eyes, a high forehead, sensuous lips and a good-natured,
ironic (some may have thought sly) smile. For this description we
are forced to rely on the memoirs of contemporaries, mostly recorded
very much later, as no portrait of Rothschild has survived. For
religious reasons, none was probably ever made. The picture pur-
portedly depicting Rothschild that is sometimes reproduced, showing a portly man of agreeable, rounded, clean shaven features, is of
dubious value. It was made years after his death by a man who
had never met him in the flesh. Contemporaries remembered him
wearing a short, pointed, black beard, a wig which, as a Jew, he was
not allowed to powder, and a three-cornered hat. But these too were
souvenirs recorded long after the event. The fact is, we do not really
know what he looked like. We do know he was hard working and
ambitious to succeed.

Selling a few old coins could not possibly make him rich. But it
was a means to establish contacts with persons of wealth, power and
importance. Such a person was the young Crown-Prince Wilhelm,
the future Landgrave of Hesse, who would play a decisive role in
Rothschild's future career. Wilhelm was the presumptive heir to his
father's vast fortune. His pedigree was one of the finest in Europe.
George III of England was his cousin. He was married to a daughter
of the King of Denmark. As Crown-Prince he was already the absolute ruler of the independent little county of Hanau, a few miles east
of Frankfurt.

Wilhelm happened to be acquainted with General von Estorff, one of young Rothschild's former clients in Hanover. At just about the time Rothschild returned from Hanover to Frankfurt, Erstorff visited Wilhelm in Hanau. It so happened that Wilhelm had just started his own coin collection. Estorff mentioned Rothschild's name to the young prince and probably introduced Rothschild to him. This first meeting between Rothschild and the young prince later became the subject of fanciful speculation. According to one story, Estorff introduced Rothschild to the Crown-Prince during a game of chess. The prince was about to lose the game when Rothschild whispered a tip in his ear and the prince won. At this point, according to the story, the prince cried: "He's no fool this man whom you've recommended to me, General!" The story may be apocryphal but it sums up, as such stories sometimes do, the central facts of the case. Rothschild was certainly no fool. The young prince, thrifty almost to the point of avarice, but shrewd, able and autocratic, appreciated ability in others, especially in money matters. He was also nearly the same age as Rothschild. Unlike others of his class, he associated with Freemasons, members of a semi-secret order which, in the spirit of French eighteenth-century enlightenment, advocated religious tolerance. He held no particular prejudice against Jews.

The first business contact between Rothschild and the Crown-Prince probably took place in Frankfurt during one of the fairs. We know from Wilhelm's accounting ledgers that in the spring of 1765 he visited the Frankfurt fair three times. His privy purse accounts for that year show an expenditure in June 1765 of "38 gulden 30 kreuzer to Jew Meyer for medals". There is little doubt he meant Rothschild. Jews at that time were commonly identified by their first names even when they had a second. (Other Jews are listed in the same accounts by their first names only.) The ledgers for 1766–70 have been lost but it seems likely that during these years Rothschild sold more coins and medals to the Crown-Prince, perhaps entire collections. Rothschild referred to these deliveries in an appeal addressed to the Crown-Prince in 1769 asking for the honorary title of a "Court-Factor". In the eighteenth century, as in ours, honors had to be solicited. Humbly, but at the same time conscious of his dignity and purpose, Rothschild wrote:

It has been my particular and high fortune to make several deliveries to Your Lofty Princely Serenity to Your Highest gracious satisfaction. I now stand ready to exert all my energies and my entire fortune to serve Your Lofty Princely Serenity whenever in future it shall please You to Command me. A special and powerful incentive to this end would be given me if Your Lofty Princely Serenity deigned to grace me with an appointment as Court-Factor. I make bold to raise this request in the conviction that by so doing I am not giving any trouble and in the hope that such distinction would lift up my commercial standing and, *coupled with other circumstances*, help me make my fortune here in the city of Frankfurt.

The letter was clearly written for Rothschild by someone else. We know from other letters in his own hand that he could not himself have managed its faultless style and courtly tone. He may have approached other princes with similar intentions. The Crown-Prince readily granted the request a few weeks later:

We, Wilhelm, by the Grace of God Landgrave and Crown-Prince of Hesse, Grand Duke of Fulda, Duke at Hersfeld, Count of Katzenelbogen, Dietz, Ziegelheim, Schaumburg & reigning Count of Hanau etc etc etc Most Graciously bestow the title of Court-Factor upon the Protected Jew Meyer Amschel Rothschild of Frankfurt.

Rothschild now hung on the door of the *Hinterpfann* a round colored shield decorated with the arms of Hesse and Hanau. At twenty-five, he was the first in his family to win a distinction for which his grandfather and great-grandfather must have striven in vain. No immediate privileges were attached to it. But in the words of a popular saying at the time "in the crush of life a title saves you from many kicks". The title did not automatically grant Rothschild the coveted right to leave the Judengasse at night or on Sundays – fourteen years would pass before he would finally attain that privilege in 1785 – and it did not release him from any of the other humiliating duties imposed in Frankfurt and elsewhere on "protected" Jews. The title was largely honorary, much like the designation in England today

"By Appointment to H.R.H. the Duke of Kent, Wine Merchants". And yet, as a first step toward becoming a Court-Jew, associated with a reigning prince, it was not entirely useless.

The "other circumstances" to which Rothschild alluded may have been his forthcoming marriage to a young woman of the Frankfurt Judengasse named Guttle Schnapper. When Rothschild declared in his letter to the prince that the title of Court-Factor would "help me make my fortune here in the city of Frankfurt", the German term for good "fortune" he used (*Glück*) implied both "fortune" and "bliss". His marriage to Guttle (later Gudule) Schnapper was celebrated on 29 August 1770. Rothschild had just reached twenty-five – the minimum legal age in Frankfurt for marriage by a Jew. The bride was seventeen. Her dowry amounted to 2,400 gulden, a considerable sum, especially by Rothschild's standards. Gudule was the daughter of Wolf Salomon Schnapper, a bill broker and money-changer and a Court-Factor himself to the little principality of Sachsen-Meiningen. The Schnappers lived a few yards down the Judengasse in a house called *Zur Eule* (At the Owl). As was the custom of the time, the marriage was an arranged one. Rothschild's receiving a title as Wilhelm's Court-Factor may have played a role in the negotiations between the two families.

The couple might have preferred a house of their own. But houses in the Judengasse rarely, if ever, became vacant. Rothschild led Guttle back to his bachelor quarters above the shop in the crowded *Hinterpfann*, which they now shared with his brothers, Moses and Calmann, and their families. In preparation for the forthcoming marriage, the distant relatives had been bought out by the brothers a few months before. Rothschild and Guttle now owned three-eighths of the house.

Guttle was a child of the ghetto who knew how to make the best of the hard conditions in the over-crowded house. Contemporaries remembered her as a tough, hard-working, thrifty woman of good sense and humor, with an instinctive intolerance of all ostentation that endured later even in great wealth. She would bear Rothschild ten children who survived and perhaps six or seven more who died at birth or soon after.

With his young wife at his side, Rothschild threw himself into his business with determination and zest. Gentlemen did not normally look for gilded curios in the muddy backyard of a tenement in the Judengasse, and Rothschild had to go to find his customers. He spent a large part of his time travelling between Frankfurt and neighboring cities. Within a day's travel from Frankfurt by stage-coach lay Darmstadt, Mainz, Wiesbaden and the capitals of other petty principalities where courtiers and rich burghers were interested in Rothschild's wares collected coins, quaint jewels, medals and other unusual items. Coins and medals also served as christening gifts and were put in children's savings-pots.

Frankfurt's great spring and autumn fairs were natural occasions for Rothschild to advance further his coin and medal business. Several art-auctions took place during the fair which attracted collectors and dealers of coins from Germany and abroad. Here, Rothschild bought and sold individual coins as well as entire collections.

Between fairs he ran something like a mail-order business. In 1771 he published the first of several printed coin catalogues which he sent out during the next twenty years at regular intervals to potential customers all over Germany. These included the King of Bavaria, the Duke of Weimar (Goethe's patron) and of course his first benefactor,

Es hat Innhaber dieses, ohne diese Münzen auch eine
Anzahl Medaillen um billige Preiße zu verkaufen.

Adresse

Mayer Amschel Rothschild,

Hoch-Fürstl. Hessen-Hanauischer Hof-Factor,
wohnhaft in Frankfurt am Mayn.

1 7 8 3.

Summe: fl. 5074, 35 x.

Between fairs, Rothschild ran something like a mail-order business. This is the last page of his catalogue for 1783, offering old coins as well as "a number of medallions at cheap prices." (*Courtesy Jewish Museum, Frankfurt.*)

Wilhelm, the Prince of Hesse and Hanau. Several of these catalogues, of ten to sixteen pages each, were still extant earlier in this century, and perhaps still are. Luxuriously bound in gold-embossed leather, some were furnished with the *ex libris* of his princely clients. Rothschild spent much time and effort on their preparation. The catalogues listed ancient "Greek, Roman and pagan" silver and gold coins as well as more recent rarities of German, Russian, French or Swedish origin. Each coin was carefully dated, visually described and identified by its number in a recent scientific handbook. Unlike coins traded in the normal exchange business, the value of rare coins and medals depended not on their silver or gold content but on their beauty, history and state of preservation. Rothschild's catalogues reflected a knowledge of numismatics, of history and perhaps even of art that he could not have acquired in the Talmud school:

> Those requiring any of these beautiful Coins, which are available at low prices, are asked to address themselves to the Owner thereof, who has more rare *Cabinet* coins for sale as well as Ancient Rarities and Antiques.

Address

Mayer Amschel Rothschild

The Lofty Prince of Hesse-Hanau's Court-Factor,

resident at Frankfurt-am-Mayn

One catalogue advertised "antique cut figures and stones, beautiful statues some with mounted diamonds; the same will be sent in, if desired, for inspection by amateurs, and the cheapest price stated". The Frankfurt commercial register and address book of 1778 listed Rothschild as the city's only Jewish dealer in "antiques, medals and objects of display". Clients were able to receive Rothschild's coins by mail; those not wanted were to be sent back by return mail at Rothschild's expense. Listed prices were not binding. The final purchase price was negotiated in writing; it could be up to 50 per cent less than the listed price. The invoice of one such transaction is preserved in the Bavarian State Archive. It shows that, in 1789, Duke Karl Theodore of Bavaria had selected eighteen rare coins out of many others sent to him by Rothschild for inspection. Instead of

Verzeichniß einer Anzahl rarer Cabinets-
thaler, nach des Herrn von Maday vollstän-
digen Thaler-Cabinet numerirt, wie auch eine Anzahl
sehr rarer Gold- und Silber-Münzen, Gold- und
Silberne Römische, Griechische, Antique, und Heyd-
nische Münzen; welche vor beystehende Preiße zu haben
sind.

527

Nro.	Röm. Kayserliche.	fl.	kr.	Nro.	dessen belorbeer-	fl.	kr.
1	ohne Jahrzahl .	4	—		tes Kopfstück von		
3	Doppelthl.von1505	10	—		der rechten Seite,		
ditto	1¹⁄₅ Loth von 1505	5	—		unten M. Revera		
2386	Doppelth.ohneJ.Z.	7	30		gratia dei sum id		
7	B. B. linke Seite				q. sum 1584. das		
	von 1518 . .	3	30		gekrönte u. in der		
ditto	Doppelthl.von1518	7	—		Länge getheilte		
14	von 1532 . . .	15	—		französische u. na-		
2395	von 1536 . . .	5	—		varrische Wappen	4	—
2396	Doppelthl.von1541	8	—		Königl. Englische.		
2410	von 1549 . . .	5	—	156	von 1551 . . .	4	30
2414	ohne Jahrzahl .	3	30	160	ohne Jahrzahl .	4	30
2424	von 1622 . . .	3	—	5248	Doppelthl.von1642	25	—
2461	von 1743 . . .	4	30	166	½ von 1644 . .	2	30
	Königl. Spanische.			168	½ von 1652 . .	1	—
68	Doppelth.ohneJ.Z.	10	—	169	von 1658 Original	12	—
6075	Der Av. und 6027			ditto	½ von 1658 . .	5	—
	Rev. Zwittertha-			ditto	½ von 1658 . .	2	—
	ler von 1586 .	6	—	5326	½ von 1702 . .	2	30
2497	Doppelthl.von1571	25	—	6120	½ von 1685 . .	6	—
2503	½ von 1588 . .	3	—	5609	½ von 1689 . .	1	40
2522	¼ von 1702 . .	1	—		K. Schottländische.		
	Königl.Französische			181	von 1566 . . .	12	—
2547	½ div. von 1578 .	1	40	184	von 1570 . . .	8	—
2548	½ von 1580 . .	1	40	ditto	von 1571 . . .	8	—
6099	½ div. von 1582 .	1	40		Kön. Schwedische.		
2554	¼ von 1610 . .	1	—	192	½ von 1540 . .	1	30
131	½ ohne Jahrzahl .	2	30	2616	von1603 eine Klippe	2	—
148	von 1613 . . .	2	30	233	von 1660 . . .	3	30
	½ ohn recensirter Thlr.			240	von 1672 . . .	7	—
	Av. Henricus II. d.			249	von 1709 . . .	4	—
	g. Rex Navarre,			258	von 1731 . . .	3	40
					A		

Rothschild's catalogue *c.* 1770, listing rare Greek, Roman, Austrian
and French gold and silver coins and their prices. (*Courtesy Jewish
Museum, Frankfurt.*)

paying the listed price of 265 gulden, the Duke paid only 153 gulden and 32 kreuzer.

He often attached personal letters to his catalogues. One such letter to F. J. Bertuch, a well known man of letters and Privy Councillor to the Duke of Weimar, is full of interest to the curious observer of Rothschild's character and approach:

> Gracious Sir, last week I had the Gratification of being able to acquire a strong coin collection from the Count von Gersdorff. At the same time the count's secretary informed me that Your Highness owns a nice collection yourself and is daily buying more coins to complete it. This encourages me to take the liberty of sending the attached Catalogus of my coins for sale. Should you chose any . . . I will immediately humbly send . . . In deepest submissiveness and in highest Consideration, I remain, respectfully, Your Lofty Highness' humblest servant
>
> Meyer Amschel Rothschild
> facteur de la Cour
> Le prince hereditaire Landgrave de Hesse
> Francfurt sur le Mayn
> *Franckfurt, 22 August 1780*

The translation does not reflect the fascinating combination of poor grammar and utter sureness and insouciance. Clearly written by Rothschild himself in pidgin German, this letter throws interesting light on his self-confidence, energy and initiative. Rothschild is perfectly aware that his German is faulty, if not atrocious, but does not hesitate to write to a leading German *littérateur*. He freely shifts from Latin to Gothic script in the same sentence and sometimes in the same word. He uses capital letters profusely even for verbs. It is not a question of high, low or inelegant German, or of incorrect spelling, as standardized spelling was introduced only much later, but of general culture, or lack of it. Rothschild's nonchalance as a letter writer is remarkable for a man who at this time was already involved in rich and varied business affairs.

He brought to his work a certain natural flair, a knowledge of human nature and a capacity to generate trust. As a rule, he preferred

to minimize profits in the hope of increasing turnover and consequently his prices were often lower that those of other dealers. He
was ready to lower them even more, at times even at a small loss, in
the hope of more profitable business in the future. He was an ardent
reader of newspapers. As a budding banker, he recognized the importance of early, and if possible, advance information of important
political events.

On 20 August 1771, the first anniversary of their wedding, Guttle
gave birth to their first child, a daughter, Schönche. Three sons,
Amschel Meyer (1773), Salomon Meyer (1774), Nathan Meyer
(1777) and two more daughters Belche (1781) and Breinliche (1784)
followed. Rothschild's affairs prospered during these years. His
declared income between 1771 and 1779 was 30,680 gulden, an
annual average of 3,835 gulden. This was nearly twice the annual
income of Frankfurt's chief magistrate, the *Schultheiss*, the city's highest paid official. It was half as much again as the annual income of the
patrician Goethe family, which amounted to 2,400 gulden. Thrifty
Guttle Rothschild spent only a fraction of this annual income on her
household; a large part was pumped back into the business.

Rothschild's brother Calmann, who took care of the exchange
shop while Rothschild travelled with his coins, was ailing and died
in 1782 at the age of thirty-five. Rothschild remained sole owner of
the business, which he continued tirelessly to enlarge. Guttle took
charge of the exchange shop, cashing and discounting bills. Rothschild took on everything else that could be traded profitably. Next
to coins and medals he sold English wools and cottons, coffee, sugar
and rabbit skins. And there were the beginnings of a banking
business. He handled capital transfers, letters of credit and granted
small loans to shopkeepers and so-called *cavaliers* (gentlemen).

The bulk of Rothschild's business was undoubtedly trade. As a
banker he was still waiting for a main chance with a princely court.
A small opportunity offered itself in Hanau in 1776. Rothschild had
been Wilhelm's honorary Court-Factor for some years, but that
appointment had led only to a few sales of medals and coins. In 1776
the enterprising Wilhelm sold a first contingent of Hessian soldiers
to his English cousin, George III, for use as cannon-fodder in the
American war. In this profitable business Wilhelm was following the

Burghers, soldiers, packhorses, maids, porters, Jewish and Christian
merchants, moneychangers, sailors, coachmen, visiting foreigners and
many others in an oil painting of Frankfurt's river port outside the *Fahrtor*.
W. F. Hirt, 1757. (*Courtesy Historical Museum, Frankfurt.*)

example of his ancestors under whose reign, as Landgraves of Hesse, the sale of soldiers had become a major export industry. The soldiers were not mercenaries, in any accepted sense of that word; they were ruthlessly pressed into service, on the Prussian model, from among the poor peasantry. Deserters were made to run the gauntlet up to twelve times, two days in a row. In a seller's market, the terms were exceedingly tough for the English customer. But George III had already been rebuffed by the Russians and the Dutch; he had no choice but accept Wilhelm's oppressive terms.

There was a base recruiting fee of fifty-one thaler (seventy-six gulden) for every foot soldier, payable within two months, and additional levies for any man killed or wounded. Three wounded men counted as one killed for whom another levy of fifty-one thaler was charged:

> If an epidemic, shipwreck, siege or battle should cause unusually high losses to a regiment or corps, the King of England will in addition liberally pay the costs of recruiting new soldiers and officers needed to restore said corps to its former strength . . . [the price of each being calculated] inclusive of recruiting and [burying the] corpse.

None of these payments benefited Hesse or the county of Hanau in any way. Like his father the Landgrave, the Crown-Prince considered the entire county his private domain. Wilhelm's net profits in 1776 from such business were estimated at several millions. Some of this money became due during the summer. It arrived in Hanau in the form of bills of exchange redeemable a few weeks later at an English bank. The bills were not subject to interest payments in case of delayed transfer. The Crown-Prince was therefore anxious to invest the money as soon as possible at the highest obtainable interest rate. He first had to convert his English bills into local currency by selling them, at a discount, to local bankers. To avoid depressing the market by cashing too much at once, sales were carefully timed or limited to small batches. Bankers where invited to bid for them in cash. For larger amounts, credit lines were offered to a limited number of trustworthy bankers.

The trade in bills was very profitable. Commissions and other fees could reach more than 10 per cent of face value. Though there is no specific record of it in the official files, there is good reason to believe that Rothschild was one of the bankers offered credit by the prince to enable them to discount his English bills at agreeable rates. This is obvious from a letter he wrote to Wilhelm in 1789, reminding him that on several occasions, in the past he, Rothschild, had succeeded in "raising the price of the English bills, for the benefit of the princely treasury, higher than it had been before, and the reason for this was that I had been granted credit".

Such cases, however, were still rare, and far apart. It is impossible now to tell why. Rothschild retained his honorary title, but try as he might, his relations with the Crown-Prince remained distant. His patience never ran out. He travelled back and forth between Frankfurt and Hanau, tirelessly making the rounds, cultivating contacts with influential officials in Wilhelm's court. Among these officials was a young man named Carl Friedrich Buderus. Buderus was a rising star in the administration of Wilhelm's treasury. Buderus was gracious to the visiting Jew – an attitude rare enough at the time – but, at this early stage, of little help otherwise.

He was luckier with another prince, Karl Anselm of Thurn and Taxis. His family – of Italian extraction – had been hereditary postmasters of the Holy Roman Empire since the sixteenth century. Karl Anselm's business headquarters were in Frankfurt. In 1780 Rothschild became one of his preferred bankers, discounting the prince's bills and granting him short term loans. The Thurn and Taxis postal service covered most of central Europe and its efficacy was proverbial (it was said that the high quality of the Thurn and Taxis postal service was more responsible for the blossoming of sentimental letters in Germany than the success of Goethe's *Sorrows of Young Werther*). Rothschild's ties with the administration of the Thurn and Taxis postal service were profitable to him in more than one way. He was a firm believer in the importance of good information. The postal service was an important source of commercial and political news. The Prince was widely thought to be paying for his monopoly as imperial postmaster by supplying the Emperor with political intelligence gained from mail that passed through his hands. He was not averse to using this intelligence himself – perhaps in conjunction with Rothschild – to make a commercial profit.

In the meantime, the struggle for and against Jewish emancipation in Germany was reaching a high pitch. "That the Jews of Rome are locked in a ghetto is less surprising", wrote the Swedish traveller F. F. Franzen, "but in a free Imperial and Commerce city like Frankfurt?" In 1781 a Prussian liberal named Christian Dohm, in his epoch-making book, *On the Civic Improvement of the Jews*, demanded that they be granted equal rights. Such audacity had been unheard of until then. A year later, in Vienna, the Emperor Joseph II – Frankfurt's historic overlord – issued an Imperial Edict on Tolerance which formally recognized Jews as "fellow human beings". Friedrich Klopstock, the romantic poet, celebrated the event in an ode hailing the Emperor for removing "the rusty irons from the wounded arms of the Jews".

In the dank stupor of Frankfurt, such harbingers of a new era still had great difficulty in gaining entry. The city senate had only recently banned as "sacrilegious" Gotthold Ephraim Lessing's seminal plea for religious tolerance, his play *Nathan the Wise*. Copies of the play's text were confiscated as blasphemous in a local book shop. Intellectuals in the city were unmoved by this event. Goethe alternated between prejudice and indifference. The philosopher Friedrich Hegel who worked in Frankfurt at this time as a tutor, was openly bigoted. He developed a line of thought on the wretchedness of the "Jewish consciousness" obscure enough to baffle his best exegetists. In "the prison of a Jewish soul" there was no place for Hegel's *Weltgeist*. The tragedy of the Jewish people was no Greek tragedy because "it aroused neither terror nor pity".

Notwithstanding the Emperor's Edict on Tolerance, the Frankfurt senate rejected all new pleas to abolish the most intolerable restriction, the prohibition to leave the ghetto on Sundays. "The emperor has spread the light of tolerance everywhere ... Only Frankfurt remains in darkness", leaders of the Jewish community complained. Yet the ghetto also showed little readiness to allow new light to enter. Elsewhere in Germany, Moses Mendelssohn's translation of the Pentateuch into German (in Hebrew script) had

had a catalytic effect on opinion, comparable to Diderot's *Encyclopedie* thirty years earlier in France. In the Frankfurt ghetto, Mendelssohn's translation and commentary were banned by the rabbis as "heretic ... [for] scoffing at the words of our sages". The spiritual ghetto was as narrow as the spatial ghetto. Forty-seven Frankfurt Jews nevertheless subscribed to the first volume. Rothschild was not one of them.

In 1783 – fourteen years after his appointment as a Court-Factor – Rothschild was finally granted one of those coveted gate passes that allowed a few privileged Jews to leave the ghetto at night and on Sundays and holidays. The volume of his business affairs with the Crown-Prince must have increased dramatically; or else Buderus, who had just been promoted again, was rendering him the first of many favors and services. For it was the Hanau treasury which had successfully intervened with the Frankfurt magistrate to grant Rothschild a gate pass. The reason it gave was that Rothschild was urgently needed in Hanau on Sundays, in connection with the marketing of English bills of exchange.

This was a sudden stroke of luck. The Frankfurt magistrate normally resented the presence of privileged Jews in the city. It only reluctantly granted court-agents exemptions from rules applied to ordinary Jews. The great Goethe himself – by now Privy Councillor to the Duke of Weimar and famous all over Europe – had only recently failed in an attempt to procure an exemption for one of his Jewish protégés, a Weimar court-agent named Lob Reis. The senator in charge of exemptions happened to be Goethe's uncle Johann Jost Textor who ruled that his famous nephew's intercession be "politely but firmly refused".

With his new liberty, Rothschild could, at long last, pursue his growing affairs more freely and without harassment at the gates of the Judengasse. The situation of non-privileged Jews in the city was not improving; indeed in some ways it was worsening. As the Holy Roman Empire of the German Nation was nearing its end, Jews were hopelessly caught up in the labyrinth of its contradictions and inexplicable absurdities. By a decision of the Frankfurt magistrate, Jews were suddenly forbidden to carry walking sticks. There was an uproar in the city when a local teacher of mathematics named Joseph

Rothschild, received permission, "on a strictly temporary basis" to live outside the ghetto in the interest of his profession. The guilds and civic captains of the city's fourteen quarters rose as one man to demand that Joseph Rothschild be returned to the ghetto where he belonged. Their protest was enunciated in a memorandum of no less than thirty-four pages folio and was granted; the teacher was ordered back into the Judengasse. If in recent years the occasional presence of Jews in the Christian city late in the afternoon on Sundays, after mass, had been quietly overlooked, they were now rounded up by the guards and fined. A "humble plea" to the magistrate – "What harm does it do to Christians if Jews who for so long have been locked up (into their congested street) breathe a little fresh air after 5 p.m. and the conclusion of mass in the Christian churches?" – was summarily rejected.

In 1784, at the age of forty, Rothschild was a moderately affluent man. His assets at this time have been estimated at 150,000 gulden. He must have had considerable cash savings. For when, at long last, in December of that year, a larger house became available in the Judengasse, he bought it for 11,000 gulden, the price of a palatial home in the Christian quarters of the city (twice as much as Goethe's father had paid for his twenty room mansion with big garden in the best part of Franfurt). Rothschild sold his three-eighths share in the *Hinterpfann* tenement for 3,300 gulden to his brother Moses, who now became sole owner of that house.

The new place was known as the "House at the Green Shield". Fourteen feet wide and thirty-eight feet long it was slightly less cramped than the old one. The house was described as "one of the best in the Judengasse". It was four stories high but still so narrow that in most rooms, beds and cupboards could be accommodated only along the side walls. It did have its own well and pump on the ground floor, a luxury at the time. The new house was not located in a dank backyard but was halfway down the Judengasse, facing the street at its widest point opposite the little bridge leading to it from the Christian city. Three narrow windows on each of the upper floors permitted light into the front rooms. The "Green Shield" was in fact the left half of a building, comprising two quite small apartments,

Rothschild's *comptoir*, his counting house or office, on the ground floor of the "Green Shield". Money was stored in the large iron chest secured by great locks. Photograph, 1927. (*Courtesy Hulton Deutsch Collection, London.*)

while the right half was known as "The Arch". A small ship was carved over the door of this adjacent house that belonged to a family named after it, Schiff, which achieved some fame in later years when one of its sons migrated to America and became a railway tycoon.

Perhaps because it was so rare an event, the sale of a house in the congested Judengasse was a ritualized affair. First, the *Schulklopper* announced the sale in the synagogue; then a public crier pronounced it in the street. The exchange itself took place in the presence of a rabbi holding a lit candle. The house did not become immediately vacant. Rothschild was able to move in only in 1786 with Guttle and their six children. In this house Guttle gave birth to four more children, Calmann Meyer (1788), Julie (1790), Henriette (1791) and Jacob Meyer (1792). "The House at the Green Shield", built in 1615, was still standing before the last war and was often photographed and described. Those who visited it early in this century agreed that "every step one took in it revealed the painful congestion in which

Frankfurt a. M. — Rothschilds Geburtshaus

The "Green Shield" (left half of the house in the center of the picture) before its restoration and enlargement in 1890, when the adjacent "house at the arch" was added to it. Fourteen feet wide and thrity-eight feet long, the house was "one of the best in the Judengasse". The enforced congestion of the Judengasse drove up prices. Rothschild paid almost twice as much for his half as Goethe's father had paid for his twenty room mansion with big garden in the best part of the city. Postcard, *c.* 1886.
(*Courtesy Jewish Museum, Frankfurt.*)

the Jews of that period were compelled to exist. Everything in the house was very narrow, and each particle of space was carefully turned to account".

From the street one entered a small vestibule. Here were the water pump and a stone stairwell. A door led into a small room with two windows, which served Rothschild and his wife Guttle as a bedroom. It held a good stock of linen, for laundry was only done six to eight times a year. Another door led to a kind of roof terrace with a few potted plants. The terrace was airy but the high ghetto wall at the bottom of the backyard blocked the view from there into the Christian town and the open fields beyond. Off this terrace was another back-room, Rothschild's *comptoir* – his "counting house" or office. Its furniture consisted of a stand-up desk with a high stool, a big wooden cupboard for papers, bills and books. A large iron chest, fitted with an enormous padlock, served for the storage of money.

The "Green Shield". From the street, one entered a small vestibule. A stone stairwell led to the family room upstairs. The door on the right led to Rothschild's and his wife's tiny bedroom.

Water pump in the vestibule, considered to be a great luxury at the time. Photographs, 1927. (*Hulton Deutsch Collection, London.*)

There were several secret shelves hidden in the walls. The kitchen was a small, narrow room with a hearth that could accommodate only one pot. Because of the difficulty in lighting a fire, a glowing piece of charcoal was kept in the hearth at all times, covered with a small screen. On the kitchen wall hung a few pewter pots and pans. A low closet held soup plates and cups.

Every recess in the walls and every free corner – behind the stairwell, under the roof and in the rooms upstairs – was used for storage. Little actual space was left for living. The ten children shared two little rooms under the roof. There was a living, or family, room, with three windows facing the street. It was called the "little green room" after the color of the upholstery on the chairs. A few holy books stood on a shelf. Guttle kept her withered bridal wreath on a little round table.

The most remarkable thing about the house were the two cellars. One was reached through a trap-door in the vestibule; the second, secret, cellar may have been built by Rothschild and was reached through a door concealed by a false wall. Anything hidden in this cellar could not easily be found during a search of the house, a feature that would prove useful in later years. An underground passage led from the secret cellar to the cellar of a neighboring house. It was possible, therefore, to pass easily and unseen from one house to another without going through the street or climbing the wall at the back.

Rothschild still travelled a great deal. With his new gate pass, he was assured free passage at all times, though not always immunity from being molested at the gate, nor dispensation from paying the special body tax levied against Jews at many custom barriers. The pass had to be renewed once a year. In 1787 the magistrate, for reason that remain unclear, changed the ground rules. Gate passes were no longer issued individually to each court-agent but collectively to a group of agents at a single time. This meant that if one court-agent travelled, the collective pass was deposited at the gate; the others had to rely on the capacity, or willingness, of capricious guards to recognize them as co-owners. The resultant harassment became unbearable. On 28 February 1787, Rothschild joined six other court-agents in a protest letter to the senate. It was the first time his signature appeared on a petition of this kind. The language was more audacious than the usual and echoed the radical ideas rampant on the eve of the revolution in France.

> As a human being every Jew has the same rights as all others and a just claim for protection by his sovereign. Unfortunately, the lower classes are still so bound to the prejudices of their fathers as to make believe that a Jew is not a human being like themselves. They mistreat Jews in all sorts of ways and some old men are pleased when his son mistreats a Jew. Even soldiers on occasion indulge in this punishable tyranny. Would they not take such a signal as an invitation for countless acts of harassment? They would take the smallest difference in clothing, hair, beards and the like as an excuse for the most stringent examinations at the city gates. At the slightest deviation it would enable them to arrest the Jew and march him off to the main guard house as a common thief.

The petition was successful, the decree was withdrawn and individual passes were once again issued. The incident highlighted the backward conditions in Frankfurt compared to those elsewhere in Germany. The Russian traveller Nikolai Karamazin passed through Frankfurt in the summer of 1789 and, though he must have seen worse in Russia, was shocked to find the inhabitants of the ghetto "locked like prisoners in their cells . . . patiently awaiting their death sentence, scarcely daring to beg their judges for mercy".

In Prussia, the emancipation had made considerably more progress. Berlin and Königsberg saw the beginnings of social exchanges and even marriages between Christians and Jews – unheard of in Frankfurt. Dulled and intimidated by habit, Jews in Frankfurt continued to suffer their oppression with little, if any, protest. Before 1796, no appeal to the senate ever demanded complete abolition of the walled ghetto. "They never demanded the removal of their chains; they were satisfied if the chains did not cut too deep", Isidor Kracauer, the historian of the Jews of Frankfurt, wrote. Revolution in Frankfurt would come from without, from France.

CHAPTER THREE

Patronage and Power

IN THE FALL OF 1785, the old Landgrave of Hesse-Kassel, Friedrich II, died of a stroke. His son Wilhelm, Rothschild's erstwhile patron, succeeded to the throne as Wilhelm IX. The new Landgrave, whose avarice was already legendary, learned with pleasure that he had inherited a colossal fortune. He was forty-two years old. Kassel, his new capital, was one of the most beautiful and luxurious in Germany. His land, Hessen, was one of the poorest and most backward principalities in the Empire; but with the fortune he had inherited from his father, the Landgrave was said to be the richest man in Europe. Torrents of gold, from the sale of soldiers to foreign sovereigns, had flowed into his father's coffers during the past twenty-five years. A large part of this money was invested in English government bonds, producing handsome profits. The remainder had been spent on great building projects, art collections and magnificent private parks. Wilhelm's fortune was variously estimated at between 40 and 120,000,000 gulden.

Kassel was a hundred miles north of Frankfurt and much farther than Hanau, which Rothschild could reach by stage coach in less than an hour. But the connection with Wilhelm was too useful and Rothschild was determined not to lose it. He redoubled his efforts to win Wilhelm's trust. Soon after Wilhelm's coronation, Rothschild travelled to Kassel to remind the new Landgrave of his existence. Then he waited. Though the Landgrave took his time, Rothschild remained in touch with Buderus and the rest of Wilhelm's treasury officials. Buderus was now chief revenue officer, in charge of Wilhelm's privy purse. He was often in Frankfurt on Wilhelm's business, and visited Rothschild there. Buderus had growing business interests of his own. His investments in bonds and in real estate seem to have

The Landgrave's palace on the Friedrichsplatz in Kassel. Rothschild
established his first branch office in Kassel. Aquarell by Johann Werner Kobold,
date unknown. (*Courtesy City Museum, Kassel.*)

been handled through Rothschild. He encouraged Rothschild to
continue his quest for a larger share of the Landgrave's business.
Rothschild certainly had the honesty and humility that princes
demanded, and energy and intelligence to boot. Buderus also warned
Rothschild that princes were capricious clients. Wilhelm was more
capricious than most. He was suspicious, careful and always took his
time. He was also greedy. Rothschild made several more trips to
Kassel to further his cause; in 1787 he was there with some fine
jewels and coins which he offered Wilhelm at "an exceptionally
low price".

The Landgrave, recognizing a bargain, took the jewels. At the
same time he gave Rothschild the impression that he might grant
him another opportunity one day to handle the conversion of his
English currency (by this time his English income alone amounted to
£250,000 a year). Then, apparently, Wilhelm forgot him. Rothschild
stood by watching, no doubt enviously, as others discounted the

Landgrave's bills; the old established Christian firms in Frankfurt – Bethmann Brothers, Preye & Jordis and Ruppel & Harnier – and the Jewish court-agent Feidel David. All were veterans of long standing and jealously guarded their positions at the Kassel court. They had dealt for decades with the Landgrave's father and with Wilhelm himself, discounting bills and negotiating their loans to foreign sovereigns. It was not easy for an outsider like Rothschild to compete with them.

Things did not immediately improve even when Buderus was promoted to a top post in the new Landgrave's financial administration. Thirty-years old, Carl Buderus was the son of a gentleman's valet. He had begun his career in Wilhelm's service at the age of sixteen as tutor to one of his illegitimate sons. In that capacity he soon convinced Wilhelm of his financial talents by presenting him with detailed plans to increase his fortune. Thus, a few months after he was hired he suggested a way to raise the net income of Wilhelm's agricultural enterprises by thousands of silver thalers through the simple device of taking into account not only that denomination but also its fractions, the groschen which was worth one-thirtieth of a thaler. This, apparently, had not occurred to anyone before. He further proposed to raise the price of salt by one kreuzer each time Wilhelm had another illegitimate child, which happened quite frequently, to support mother and child in style. Fantastic estimates of the number of such offspring circulated. According to one version, there were seventy.

Buderus was a good administrator and his master's loyal servant, but after he married he was in need of money. It was not unusual for underpaid public officials to engage in private business ventures on the side and Wilhelm was fully aware of this. With Rothschild's help, Buderus's private investments produced handsome profits. Buderus promised Rothschild he would intercede for him and, in 1789, Rothschild wrote again to remind the Landgrave of his past services:

> I flatter myself that as a Princely Hessian Court-Factor of long standing I should not be regarded [in Kassel] as a stranger . . . the revenue office [Buderus] will be my witness that I have always been prompt in my payments.

Rare coins and gold medallions supplied to the Bavarian court by
Rothschild, 1789. (*Courtesy Jewish Museum, Frankfurt.*)

He asked the Landgrave for a larger share in the bills business,
promising to "pay the highest price offered by anyone in Kassel".

The Landgrave was more responsive to this than he had been to
previous appeals in the past. Buderus also kept his promise and put
in a good word. As a first step, the Landgrave ordered a report on
Rothschild's reputation and financial assets. How reliable was he?
How large were his assets? How good was his credit? The report on
Rothschild's reputation was exceedingly good; he always paid the
highest prices, was punctual in paying his debts and thus deserved

to be given credit. But the Landgrave's officials were unable to form a clear picture of Rothschild's financial reserves. The Jewish community assessment lists were consulted. They showed that over the previous fifteen years Rothschild had paid taxes on assets totalling only 2,000 gulden. Moreover, there was little, if any, visible wealth. The family's modest lifestyle did not reflect the true extent of Rothschild's accumulated riches, which he continued to channel back into the business. This, coupled with Rothschild's inborn compulsion to hide his still modest wealth, undermined his own purpose. (Long after his death one of his sons quoted him as saying: "Something three people know about is no more a secret".)

The result was that the Landgrave decided to move very slowly. Rothschild was tentatively granted credit for only £800. At the same time, his main competitor, the Kassel court-agent Feidel David, was authorized £25,000 on six months' credit. A few months later, Rothschild applied once more asking for £10,000 in credit. The Landgrave, who personally approved every transaction, authorized only £2,000.

Over the next few years, although Buderus continued to recommend him, Rothschild's involvement in the business affairs of the Landgrave barely increased. However, his other affairs flourished as never before. He was able to rent more storage space outside the ghetto. His two older sons, Salomon and Amschel – fifteen- and sixteen-years old respectively – joined him in the business. With three able men working from morning until late at night Rothschild was now a major wholesaler with large stocks of wool, cotton cloth and flour. As a result of the revolution in France, the price of flour was at its highest level since the Middle Ages.

While the revolution was gaining momentum in France, the two annual Frankfurt fairs continued as before. The luxury market had collapsed but exceptionally high prices could be charged for commodities. Rothschild's pass enabled him to leave the Judengasse on business even when, after the death of Joseph II in 1790, the ghetto gates were locked for the coronation of Leopold, the new Holy Roman Emperor. The colorful procession of princes wound its way through the streets and the cannons thundered from the walls. As the bearer of a gate pass Rothschild was entitled to watch the processions as long as he remained tactfully in the rear, behind a pillar or the window of a house. It is improbable that he availed himself of this privilege. He travelled constantly and was now able to rent even more storage space outside the ghetto.

Between the fall of the Bastille and the execution of Louis XVI, Frankfurt twice re-enacted its grand imperial show, as though nothing had changed: Leopold II was crowned Emperor in 1790 and upon his death two years later, the next Emperor, Francis II, was enthroned. On this second occasion, the last in the history of the Holy Roman Empire, Landgrave Wilhelm of Hesse, Rothschild's hesitant patron, was also in Frankfurt, lavishly entertaining the assembled noblemen and electors. His army lay outside the walls to protect them.

Fewer than ten weeks later, on 22 October 1792, troops of the French revolution, under General de Custine, appeared outside Frankfurt's walls. Wilhelm, whom the French accused of selling the blood of his subjects to fill his own purse, withdrew to Kassel trembling for his fortune and his crown. Frankfurt capitulated without a fight. The tricolor was raised on the arsenal outside the northern gate leading into the Jewish ghetto. The French general imposed a fine of 2,000,000 gulden on the city for having granted asylum in Frankfurt to a small number of fleeing French aristocrats.

In nearby Mainz and in the Rhineland, Jews were welcoming the French troops as liberators, for it was only a year earlier that France had granted French Jews full civil rights. But in the Frankfurt ghetto, the French were met with hostility and condemned as foreign aggressors. The Jews of Frankfurt felt (or at least feigned) a love for the city that had humiliated and oppressed them but which for them had been a home of sorts since the thirteenth century. When, a few weeks later, the small French garrison was forced out by Prussian troops, the Judengasse erupted with cries of "Down with the French" and "Long live the king of Prussia". (Goethe's mother could afford to be more enlightened. With the indifference of an eighteenth-century patrician to the new nationalism, she wrote to her son: "It's all the same to me. Whether the French control this side of the Rhine or the other does not disturb me while I eat or sleep". She preferred the presence of French troops "to wooden Prussians".) The Judengasse, by contrast, erupted in demonstrations of patriotism. The French commander went so far as to claim that one of the reasons for his capitulation was the hostility shown to his troops by the Jews of Frankfurt.

Wilhelm of Hesse had been wavering for some time between remaining neutral, in the interest of his business, or joining the grand coalition against revolutionary France, in the interest of his crown. He now joined the grand coalition on condition that England grant him a subsidy of £100,000. "Rothschild and his rivals were kept fully occupied in discounting the bills received from England in connection with this subsidy."

Rothschild's business was moving ahead in other ways too. It now also included a transportation and forwarding agency. His sons were throwing themselves into the work with imagination and verve, surpassing their father's fondest hopes. For the first time, hired help was available in the house to write letters, run errands, carry heavy loads and chop wood for the stoves. The English–Prussian–Austrian war against revolutionary France was relentlessly sucking Frankfurt into the maelstrom of international affairs. The large armies assembling nearby provided a natural market for enterprising business men. The Austrian commissary-in-chief, General von Wimmer, settled more or less permanently in Frankfurt to provide Austrian troops with the provisions they required. He could not meet the demands made on him alone. Wages had to be paid out regularly to Austrian soldiers stationed in different locations and fresh fodder had to be provided for their horses. Rothschild secured a contract to supply the Austrian army with wheat, uniforms, packhorses and other equipment. In addition, he was to arrange the regular distribution of soldiers' wages.

His commitments under the contract were large. To meet them he went into partnership with two other businessmen in the Judengasse, Wolf Low Schott and Beer Nehm Rindskopf. The Austrian army contract must have involved considerable capital transfers, probably of millions of gulden. That Rothschild was entrusted with so formidable a task was an indication of his growing reputation as an organizer and a businessman. To procure great quantities of war supplies – food, saddles, uniforms, tents – and deliver them quickly at

Austrian troops on the Fischerfeld outside the Judengasse. Rothschild's
profits as a pay-agent and supplier of fodder to the Austrian military
provided his first major capital accumulation. Oil Painting, anonymous, 1797.
(*Courtesy Historical Museum, Frankfurt.*)

competitive prices was a formidable task. It implied buying up and transporting as quickly as possible, often through sub-contractors, all the available food products of a province. In a pre-modern economy, businessmen like Rothschild and his partners were uniquely suited for such an undertaking. Rindskopf was his relative. Together they were able to depend on trustworthy credit and supply networks and reliable family contacts.

To maintain them, Rothschild and his sons were constantly travelling. And although they also endured losses during this period, their profits as military contractors were big enough to form their first major capital accumulation. The written records are lost, but after being assessed for ten consecutive years at only 2,000 gulden annually, in 1795 Rothschild was suddenly assessed at double that sum, 4,000 gulden. Though these figures do not necessarily reflect his entire fortune, they do give an idea of sudden, dramatic growth.

In October of 1795, Rothschild's daughter and eldest child, Schönche, married Benedikt Moses Worms, the son of another rich court-agent in the Judengasse. For the second time, the Rothschild family was entering the closed marriage circuit of the Court-Jews. Schönche received a dowry of 5,000 gulden and two years free board and lodging at the "Green Shield". Furthermore, although as a rule only sons inherited, Rothschild displayed "fatherly good-will" and promised Schönche one half of a son's current share in the inheritance, in this case 10,000 gulden. Families who made such grand provisions for their children could not hope to conceal their real incomes for long. It was little wonder that only one year later, in 1796, Rothschild's assessment was nearly quadrupled – to 15,000 gulden, the maximum taxable amount in Frankfurt. His total assets were undoubtedly very much higher.

So much money flowed through his coffers – or perhaps his book-keeping was careless – that almost a full year passed before he noticed that one of his porters, a young man named Hersch Liebmann, was systematically dipping into his cash box and stealing gold and silver coins and other valuables. Rothschild was unable to state precisely the number of missing coins and medals. He estimated his losses in louis d'or, thaler and antique medals at thirty thousand gulden, but could produce proof for only a few thousand.

But for the accidental visit of a stranger, the theft might not have been discovered at all. The interrogation and trial of the delinquent, his parents and friends dragged on for years. The surviving protocols extend over almost 500 pages folio – half as many again seem to have been lost. The court record is as evocative as a novel of daily life in the Judengasse and in the Rothschild household: both "below stairs" and upstairs in the living room and *comptoir*. It is obvious from the court record that conditions in the house and *comptoir* were lively and often chaotic, with people constantly coming and going. Clients, relatives and small children jostled for space in the narrow rooms. Large amounts of money were brought in and taken out. Goods were stored in the cellars and upstairs in the family rooms. There was no regular stock-taking and books were haphazardly kept.

The delinquent was a temporary employee, working as Rothschild's porter and handyman. The record describes him as a *Knecht* (servant or bondman). His working day included chopping wood, helping in the kitchen and going out on important errands for Rothschild and his sons. Rothschild entrusted him with large sums of money. He carried sacks of gold and silver coins up and down the stairs and, as Rothschild's messenger, to business partners and Austrian army units throughout the region. He was ambitious – and underpaid. Just as the Landgrave allowed Buderus to do business on the side, so Rothschild allowed Liebmann to augment his salary by a little buying and selling. Liebmann worked long hours, eight or nine a day for Rothschild and an additional three or four on his own. He often accompanied Rothschild on his trips. He even sold some hay to Rothschild himself and to Rothschild's main client, the Austrian army. Rothschild saw nothing unusual in this and even granted Liebmann an occasional small loan. Liebmann was having an affair with the house-maid next door. He was looking forward to marrying her and becoming an independent businessman. He invested his small savings in treasury notes, hoping to save enough over a few years to acquire a right of residence, if not in Frankfurt where prices were high and the lists closed, then perhaps elsewhere.

Before entering service with Rothschild, Liebmann seems to have been a "wandering Jew" – a man too poor to obtain permanent right of residence in Frankfurt or anywhere else in the German lands.

Jews could nowhere obtain the right of permanent residence unless they had enough money to buy a house; even when they had enough money, the *numerus clausus* applied almost everywhere. Waiting lists were long. Thousands of homeless Jews roamed the countryside like gypsies, surviving as beggars and peddlers. Some were bandits organized into gangs. The criminal argot of eighteenth-century Germany was larded with Hebraisms. Legend has it that there were pious Jewish bandits who robbed only on weekdays and on the Sabbath rested from their labours. Homeless Jews, Jewish bandits and Court-Jews shared a defiance of the society that rejected or oppressed them – the bandits through violence, the Court-Jews through flattery, artfulness and cunning.

The record does not say how Liebmann came to work for Rothschild. The Judengasse was a kind of welfare state in miniature, offering free medical assistance to the poor and alms to needy widows and orphans under the auspices of a welfare board. Rothschild headed this board, a role for which he was often lauded. The board would, on occasion, offer aid to homeless Jews roaming outside the city walls. Rothschild may have first met the wayward Liebmann under its auspices. Liebmann had to be bonded to Rothschild or he would not have been allowed to live in Frankfurt. His wages were thirty gulden a year, or two-and-a-half gulden a month. He received his meals in the house, but could not sleep there for lack of space and so shared a rented room with five others elsewhere in the Judengasse. The rent in the Judengasse was exorbitantly high and left him with a monthly income of only one-and-a-half gulden. This meant earnings of only ten pfennig a day, half the daily wage of an unskilled farmhand. For ten pfennig Liebmann could buy twelve ounces of flour, or six ounces of meat, or one measure of beer.

The suspicion of theft arose one evening when a strange man knocked on Rothschild's door asking for Liebmann, who was not at home. The man returned the following day. Rothschild engaged him in conversation. What was his business with Liebmann? The man at first hedged. Then he said that he was a broker and that Liebmann had recently bought a treasury note through him for 1,000 louis d'or. This information, as Rothschild later told the investigating judge, startled him. One thousand louis d'or (some 9,000 gulden) seemed a huge sum for a man who earned only two-and-a-half gulden a month. The broker became fearful that he might be accused of being an accessory to a crime. Upon further questioning, he confessed that Liebmann had urged him to keep their relationship secret. He was to say only that the two were only buying and selling hay and a few bales of sackcloth together.

Rothschild told the investigating judge that he had been aware that Liebmann was doing business on the side. Almost everybody in the Judengasse dealt in something or other. The lowliest *Knecht* in the Judengasse envisioned himself a businessman and Liebmann was no exception. Rothschild remembered seeing some gold coins and silver spoons which Liebmann was trying to sell. And he knew that Liebmann was supporting "wretchedly poor" parents who squatted somewhere in the neighbouring village of Bockenheim. An immediate stock taking in his office confirmed that gold medals and gold and silver coins, a diamond studded ring and other valuable antiques were missing. Rothschild was unable to state their exact value since the stock taking was not yet over. He spoke vaguely of a possible loss of 30,000 gulden.

Liebmann was arrested. Treasury notes and cash was found on him and in his parents' shack; also found were some silver spoons, a gold salt pot, a gold mug and seven medals that were returned to Rothschild without much ado. One day after Liebmann's arrest, his father appeared at Rothschild's door to plead for his son's release. Rothschild gave the investigating judge an emotional account of their meeting. The father first insisted on his son's complete innocence. Then he confessed that his son had recently given him 1,000 gulden to hide under the stove. These, and another 500 in cash, he offered Rothschild if he would withdraw his complaint and allow Liebmann to go free.

The father was arrested as an accomplice. The police suspected the existence of a crime ring. Liebmann's mother and brother and several of their contacts in neighbouring towns and villages were interrogated at length and confronted with their conflicting statements. Liebmann's parents, according to the protocol, had the reputation of being "wanton thieves". Liebmann's grandfather on his mother's side, had even had "his ear cut off" as punishment for stealing a horse. Liebmann's father was a beggar but apparently had recently bought himself a new set of blue and black clothes, a hat and gold watch. He had married off his daughter with a dowry of 500 gulden.

The cumbersome investigation dragged on with a thoroughness and pedantry astounding at a time when children were summarily hanged for stealing a loaf of bread. Each interrogation, every house search, was minutely recorded. Protocols were compared and commented upon. Liebmann, pleading his innocence, remained in jail. The investigating judge continued his plodding inquiries. Two years after his arrest, Liebmann broke down and confessed the theft of some 3,000 gulden.

He told the investigating judge that one afternoon, a year before his arrest, he had been standing by the door in the small *comptoir* in Rothschild's house. Rothschild's son Salomon and several clients were also in the room, talking. Inside the large cupboard, which was never locked, Liebmann said, there were several sacks filled with silver coins. They were the standard sacks often used in the business, each containing 1,000 gulden. He himself had carried them in a few days earlier. While Salomon was busy talking with the guests, he, Liebmann, on a sudden impulse, picked up "a couple" of sacks of money and walked out of the room. Nobody noticed what he had done. Salomon and his guests went on talking. It all happened in broad daylight. Outside in the street nobody paid much attention as he carried the sacks up to his room. People in the Judengasse were accustomed to seeing him with sacks of money. His room mates were out. He hid the sacks in a wooden box under his bed. There the money remained for almost a year, he claimed, until a few weeks before his arrest when a new room mate arrived. He did not trust the newcomer and took the money to his parents in Bockenheim. His mother stored it under her bed. Liebmann insisted he had stolen at most only 3,000 gulden of Rothschild's money.

The investigating judge asked: "Your parents did not ask where so much money had come from?" Liebmann replied: "They asked if the money had been obtained by honest means". His answer had been that he had earned it in an unusually successful business transaction. His parents knew that he had been dealing in hay. Rothschild also knew, Liebmann insisted. Rothschild had even loaned him nine carolins to finance one of his transactions.

The pre-trial investigation continued for at least another year. The authorities searched for accomplices. Every two months or so Liebmann was hauled up from his cell and questioned again. By now he was "more dead than alive", according to the protocol. After a while, he revoked his earlier confession that he had taken a couple of money sacks; he now insisted that he had stolen a little at a time over a long period. Then he changed his version again.

Only the record of Liebmann's pre-trial investigation has survived. We do not know his subsequent fate. There is little doubt that he was found guilty and may well have been hanged. Others were certainly hanged for lesser crimes. Rothschild took the affair very seriously. It was probably not so much the material loss he had suffered as the shame at having been so careless and the humiliation of betrayal by a man he had trusted and perhaps even liked. He could not be sure exactly how much he had lost and stubbornly pressed on with his own private inquiry. The official investigation was delayed by the fact that Bockenheim, although only a few miles out of Frankfurt, was in the Landgravate of Hesse, a foreign state. For every interrogation in a neighboring village, legal assistance had to be requested in writing from the local authorities, and the results of these investigations became available only after considerable delay. Rothschild impatiently rushed out to Bockenheim himself, playing detective, interrogating Liebmann's mother and rushing back to Liebmann's cell in the Frankfurt jail to confront him with her statements.

It was around this time, apparently, that he suffered another deep personal humiliation, or "molestation", walking in the street dressed "in his old-fashioned Jewish garb". It may have been another instance of *Jud mach mores!* – step aside, remove your hat and bow humbly to some ruffians. He remained conscious of his precarious condition as a Jew. He could also, however, treat unpleasantness with humor. A street urchin yelled after him "Jude!" Rothschild calmly reached into his pocket and gave him some money asking only that he repeat the cry again and again. The lad willingly cried "Jude! Jude!" Several others joined in. Rothschild watched them wistfully and recited the old Jewish blessing "Blessed be he who gave his people the Torah".

He shunned all conspicuous displays of wealth. As his wealth increased so did the modesty of his dress. People who later wrote about him noted his good nature, his charitableness and his generosity. He gave to the poor of all faiths. He liked children. The radical German writer Ludwig Boerne, himself a native of the Judengasse, wrote that the poor often crowded behind Rothschild in the streets, "like a court, masses of poor people to whom he gave alms . . . If one saw a row of beggars in the street looking pleased and comforted, one knew that the old Rothschild had just passed through. When I was a little boy I was passing with my father through the Judengasse and we ran into the old Rothschild coming out of the synagogue. Rothschild spoke first to my father. He then addressed a few kind words to me and placed his hand on my head to bless me . . . thanks to this blessing, and although I became a German writer, the cash in my pocket never completely ran out".

Another writer noted that like many other Jews, Rothschild "believed that God best rewards those acts of charity for which the donor received no thanks. He often walked at night through the Judengasse, pressed a few coins into the palms of all who seemed poor and hurried on in the dark".

Rothschild attended synagogue almost every day and liked conversing with Talmud scholars. Learned men from one of the three Frankfurt rabbinical seminaries often dined at his table. He was very orthodox in his religious observance but, according to contemporaries, tolerant of others who were not.

He worked long hours but also knew how to relax. He took long walks. In the mid-1790s, residents of the ghetto were finally allowed out on Sundays after five p.m., to enjoy the fresh air on one of the new promenades. (They were confined, however, to a single promenade and had to reach it through a certain gate only.) In Vienna, to which he travelled as a military contractor, Rothschild was free to walk anywhere at all times. He was denounced, however, for playing cards in a private house – gambling was illegal in Vienna as well as in Frankfurt – and was fined 700 thaler for his crime.

His business continued to thrive. He had become a major importer of English cloth into Germany. In 1795 he hired, for the first time, a young woman to handle his German and English correspondence and, under the impact of Liebmann's theft, a professional book-keeper. Until then, Schönche and his daughter-in-law Eva had taken care of the books. The new book-keeper was a young man fluent in five languages named Seligmann Geisenheimer. Rothschild's German was still rudimentary. Geisenheimer was a native of Bingen in the Rhineland, which had recently been annexed by France. As a French citizen, he was exempt from all the limitations that still applied to Frankfurt Jews. Geisenheimer could leave the Judengasse at will and live in a decent house in the Christian town.

Geisenheimer was a Freemason, though the only non-Jewish members in his lodge ("L'Aurore") were Frenchmen. A disciple of Mendelssohn and Pestalozzi, he was interested in Jewish educational reform, and in the introduction of secular studies. At a time when all reform was anathema in the ghetto and condemned by the rabbis as heresy, he supported, no doubt scandalously, the reform of the Jewish religion itself. His appointment as Rothschild's chief book-keeper suggests that the atmosphere in the orthodox Rothschild household was also beginning to change.

Other dramatic changes were underway. In May 1796, Napoleon Bonaparte defeated the Austrians at Lodi. In June the French army was again outside Frankfurt's walls, laying siege to the Austrian garrison within. A heavy cannon barrage directed at the Austrian arsenal missed its target and struck the nearby Judengasse instead. Fires raged in the narrow street for almost twenty-four hours. One-hundred-and-nineteen houses, almost half of the Judengasse, were totally destroyed; an additional twenty-one were badly damaged. Rothschild's house was among those spared. It had been empty during the bombardment. Fearing pillage and rape, the inhabitants of the Judengasse had sought refuge across the river, at Sachsenhausen, taking with them whatever could be salvaged from their locked houses. Goethe's mother criticised their impudence: "This was the tragedy of the Judengasse", she wrote to her son, "everything was emptied, hardly one living being remained inside, the folly went so far that they had put large locks on each empty house. When the fire started nobody could get into the [burning] locked houses and there were no Jews there to put out the fires."

The Judengasse burning behind the ghetto wall after the
French cannon barrage of 13 July 1796. Engraving, anonymous.
(*Courtesy Historical Museum, Frankfurt.*)

Almost 2,000 inhabitants of the Judengasse were homeless. To
accommodate them, the senate was forced to suspend the decree
forbidding Jews to live in the Christian city. For those whose houses
had not burned completely the old prohibition on leaving the street
at night and Sunday morning remained on the books, but was only
sporadically enforced. The permits enabling the homeless to live
anywhere in the city were limited to six months. However, few, if
any, of the displaced made any preparations to rebuild their old
homes. Nor did the senate force them to do so, now that the French
tricolor was flying over the city.

The French clamped a crushing war contribution on the defeated
city of up to 2 per cent of individual assets. On the list of assessed
taxpayers, Rothschild figured as the tenth richest man in the Judengasse. His declared fortune of 60,000 gulden was still far behind that
of the richest man, a banker named Michael Speyer, who declared a
fortune of 420,000 gulden.

Few people foresaw that the fire of 14 June had destroyed the ghetto forever. Rothschild acted as though it had. Even before the fire, he had been able to rent limited storage space for his wares outside the ghetto; he now moved out the remainder of his stores. Guttle Rothschild and the smaller children were finally given unrestricted use of the house. The new business premises, at Schnurgasse 21, a few minutes walk from the old ghetto, were rented from a leather merchant named Trautwein.

In November 1796, a few months after the fire, Rothschild's eldest son Amschel married. The bride, Eva Hanau, was seventeen and came from a family of court-agents. The pattern of court-agents intermarrying, established by Rothschild's own marriage to Guttle and by Schönche's to Moses Worms, was continuing. On the day of Amschel's marriage, Rothschild gave him a gift of 30,000 gulden, most probably in the form of a share in the business. Until this time, Amschel had simply been his father's faithful assistant. He now became a junior partner, under his father, in a jointly owned company.

The partnership was soon extended to Salomon and Nathan, Rothschild's second and third sons. All shared in profits and losses. Estimates of Rothschild's assets at this time vary. The lowest has been 60,000 gulden, the highest 490,000 thousand. Rothschild's original *Inventarium* (balance sheet) for 1797, recently discovered in a Moscow archive among family files confiscated by the Nazis in Vienna in 1938, confirms the higher estimate. The Moscow *Inventarium* is in the form of a little booklet, bound in green cardboard, embossed with the letters MAR in gold. It lists Rothschild's active and passive positions in 1787 and concludes with the words, apparently in his hand, "Saldo von meinen Vermögen, Gottlob, 471,221 fl" (Balance of my fortune, thank God, 471,221 gulden). The money, of course, was invested in the business. It did not include the shares of the three sons, which may have amounted to half as much again.

The detailed *Inventarium* of 1797 reflects the nature of his affairs and the diversity of his main business partners, debtors as well as creditors. They were located in Frankfurt and in most other German market-places, in Vienna, Paris, Amsterdam and London. Wilhelm IX, Landgrave of Hesse-Kassel, is absent from the list, which suggests the existence of another balance sheet. There are other interesting names, including the heads of several rich patrician families in Frankfurt. Some of Rothschild's biggest creditors at this time were becoming silent partners, or "investors" in his company. The well known art collector Johann Friedrich Stadel (after whom Frankfurt's leading art museum is named) had 70,000 gulden invested in Rothschild's firm, producing for him a nice annual profit. More modestly, but auguring things to come, another investor in Rothschild's firm was Carl Buderus (2,000 gulden).

Buderus had recently been promoted to the post of Wilhelm's Paymaster-General. This made him the most powerful treasury official in Kassel. Buderus helped Rothschild to another big breakthrough with the Landgrave: negotiating one of the Landgrave's loans to the city of Frankfurt. Rothschild's profits on this occasion may have been minimal. He had underbid everybody else in Frankfurt. But for the first time he was entering a field from which he had until now been excluded.

By 1798, four able men were at work at the firm, Rothschild and his three grown up sons. Ten-year-old Calmann and six-year-old Jacob still attended school. For little Jacob's general education, Rothschild hired a reform-minded private tutor named Michael Hess. None of the other boys had had a private tutor of Dr Hess's quality. His introduction to the household, perhaps at the liberal Geisenheimer's suggestion, reflected Rothschild's new social condition and the subtle change in his ambitions for his sons. The appointment of Hess (a future leader of the German Jewish Reform Synagogue) as tutor to his youngest son suggests that in his later years Rothschild grew considerably less orthodox in his religious outlook.

Of the grown-up sons at this time, Nathan was perhaps the ablest. At twenty-one, he was imaginative, industrious, energetic and known for his independent mind. The relaxed chaos of years past was giving way to a certain order, gently imposed by Geisenheimer. At the new headquarters in the Schnurgasse, Belche and Eva alternated as cashiers, listing all the sums received or paid out on loose sheets of paper. At the end of the day, the sheets were turned over to Geisenheimer. The bulk of the business was still trade, not banking and more and more of it was in English imports. Young Nathan was in charge of this. He dealt with the English commercial travellers who passed through Frankfurt with their wares.

In 1798, Nathan had a confrontation with one of these travelling salesmen who acted as though all of Europe depended on his good will. Nathan was incensed at the man's arrogance. He resolved to go to England himself and buy the products of that country without the cost and inconvenience of unpleasant middlemen. He also felt constrained by a dominant father and two elder brothers:

> There was not room enough for all of us in Frankfurt. I dealt in English goods ... [the travelling salesman behaved as though he] did us a favour if he sold us goods. Somehow I offended him and he refused to show me his patterns. This was on a Tuesday. I said to my father: I will go to England. I could speak nothing but German. On the Thursday I started.

Nathan related the incident forty years later, at a dinner party in the home a friend, Sir Thomas Buxton. The truth may have been slightly less dramatic. Rothschild's business with England was growing very rapidly. The decision to send Nathan was a strategy carefully thought out by Rothschild himself. It had ripened over time in discussion with his sons. Nathan was sent on his way with a capital of no less than £20,000 (some US$1,500,000 in current values), nearly half of the Rothschilds' joint assets at this time. Only a fraction was Nathan's own. The rest was company funds. The entire sum may not have been transferred at once. But the fact that so much was available and that Nathan was given custody of it indicated how profitable the business had become in recent years and the trust Rothschild placed in his twenty-one-year-old son. Rothschild's chief book-keeper, Geisenheimer, who spoke English accompanied Nathan to England; his task was to help him settle properly. Rothschild was establishing his first foreign branch.

"Life and Death" of the *Fahrtor*, with its notorious *Judensau*. The gate (and the *Judensau*) were dismantled in 1802. Engraving, date unknown. (*Courtesy Historical Museum, Frankfurt.*)

CHAPTER FOUR

A European Family

IN THE FIRST YEARS of the new century Rothschild achieved much of what he had set out to do. He expanded his banking firm and succeeded, for the first time, in negotiating several large state loans, for which government bonds served as collateral. Despite a relatively small capital basis compared to his main competitors – the older Frankfurt banks of the Bethmann Brothers, Ruppel & Harnier and Preye & Jordis – Rothschild's emerged as one of the leading houses in the city and the Landgrave's main international banker.

The competition was fierce and elicited deep passions on all sides. It was said that "Ruppel & Harnier hated Rothschild and the latter feared them". Alexander Dietz, author of a multi-volume history of trade and banking in eighteenth- and nineteenth-century Frankfurt, wrote of an "embittered battle from which Rothschild emerged as victor. Its [cruel] details were material for a drama".

Rothschild owed his success to the continuing intercession of Buderus on his behalf and to the fact that he himself was more outgoing and quick witted than his competitors. He was invariably more generous and offered better terms. He practised his old policy of maximizing volume by minimizing profits. His competitors, who for decades had handled the affairs of the landgraves of Hesse, were gradually squeezed out. By 1807 Rothschild enjoyed a near-monopoly.

The Landgrave did not give Rothschild access to his money on a whim. He was a shrewd businessman, headstrong, cold, cunning and unyielding, who knew where his best interests lay. Wilhelm tended to leave the administration of his country to his underlings; his fortune he preferred to administer himself. By 1800 it amounted to at least 45,000,000 gulden. His collection of old masters and rare coins (many of which Rothschild had supplied) was one of the finest in Germany. It was rumored that he kept an abacus on the night table by his bed and personally approved every expenditure in his household.

He spent hours each day poring over his accounts and consulting with Buderus and other financial aides. Buderus had reached the highest rank of War Counsellor. His main task was to oversee the Landgrave's foreign investments and loans. Before 1800, most of the loans the Landgrave had granted to foreign rulers were contractual and secured by guarantees in the form of preferential debentures or mortgaged real estate. After 1800, he lost his faith in debentures; most of his surpluses were invested in state bonds, while the bulk of his liquid money was on deposit in Amsterdam and London. In his vaults in Kassel he kept ready, for profitable use, large sums of cash, up to several million gulden. Under an assumed name he even ran a loan company that offered mortgages to small shopkeepers, bakers and shoemakers in Hesse.

At the age of fifty-seven, Rothschild was able to look with some satisfaction on the results of forty years of hard work. He was not the richest man in Frankfurt, nor even in the Judengasse, but he was rich and charitable enough to be counted as one of the more prominent men in the community. His success was not limited to a single branch of business. In addition to his bank, his trade in textiles, colonial goods, coins and antiquities, he also traded in wine, a business only recently opened to Jews.

He was proud of his children. Nathan was prospering in England. Amschel and Salomon were at his side, working in the business, as were his daughters Belche and Breinliche and Amschel's wife Eva. No one in the family was idle. The women occupied positions of trust in the *comptoir*. The fourth son, Calmann, was twelve; within a year or so he too would be given work in the warehouse or office. Like his elder brothers, he had been apprenticed to it since an early age. The fifth, Jacob was only eight and still in the *heder*.

In a joint patent issued in Vienna on 29 January 1800, the Habsburg Emperor Franz II appointed Rothschild and Amschel his Imperial Crown-Agents. The Emperor normally handed out this distinction about six or seven times a year; a double appointment was rare. It reflected the Rothschilds' growing reputation in Vienna.

An "Imperial" appointment sounded grander than the minor Hessian title Rothschild had carried so far. Father and son had, of course, solicited their new titles in writing and lobbied for them among their acquaintances at the Vienna court. The titles came with new liberties, most notably the right to bear arms ("rifles, pistols as well as swords"). Rothschild perhaps hoped that they would help overcome their remaining handicap as disenfranchised Jews.

The elaborate patent – "We, Franz II, by the Grace of God elected Roman Emperor, at all times Augmentor of the Reich, King in Germany, Hungary, Bohemia etc etc" – paid homage to the services Rothschild had rendered the Emperor during the recent war against France. It noted his reputation as an upright and honest businessman and ceremoniously called upon all the Emperor's vassals to guarantee the two Rothschilds, their families and dependants, free and safe passage everywhere in the Holy Roman Empire of the German Nation, on land and water, "exempt from all levies, poll-taxes and other surcharges imposed on [their] co-religionists".

If this seemed to be a kind of super-passport, as Rothschild hoped, it soon transpired that it was little more than a piece of paper. On the eve of its final dissolution, the Holy Roman Empire was itself a paper empire. Local bureaucrats challenged its documents and their bearers at will. We know that on at least one occasion, Rothschild's new imperial diploma was of little use to him. A year after receiving it, he was travelling in a stage-coach from Frankfurt to Berlin. At Butzbach, on the border of Hesse-Kassel and Hesse-Darmstadt, he was requested by a customs officer to pay the obligatory Jews' body tax. Rothschild presented his diploma. After some argument, he was granted an exemption. But the customs officer was later reprimanded for his "mistake". Rothschild was formally charged with a "crime" and ordered to pay the levy retroactively.

Nevertheless, he continued to solicit additional honors. They were an added precaution in uncertain times; or, perhaps, he was still bound emotionally by an older world where the only way to overcome insult and discrimination led through a prince's court. Titles were also, of course, a form of commercial recommendation, thought to inspire confidence and trust. More than anything, perhaps, Rothschild needed to reassure himself.

On 26 November 1800, his second son Salomon married eighteen-year-old Caroline Stern, the only daughter of Jacob Heyum Stern, a wine wholesaler. As usual, Rothschild had a hand in choosing the bride. The *kethuba* (marriage contract) stipulated a large dowry and two years' room and board at the home of the bride's father, a few doors away in the Judengasse. Caroline joined the other women in the *comptoir*. Relatives were less expensive and more reliable than strangers.

At about this time, Rothschild made a subtle change to his first name. Until now, it had been the Hebrew "Meyer". As of 1802, we find him signing his name "Mayer", which perhaps sounded more German. His sons continued to collect titles, which they must have come to recognize in the end with a kind of ironic pleasure. On 15 January 1802, the Landgrave appointed Salomon and Amschel honorary Pay-Office-Agents in his war treasury. Salomon joined the local French-speaking masonic lodge "L'Aurore". A year later, the Landgrave promoted Rothschild to the rank of *Oberhofagent* (Chief Court-Agent) – the highest position in the Kassel hierarchy of Court-Jews – though only after Rothschild had paid him one hundred louis d'ors for the honor. The Prince of Thurn and Taxis, the empire's hereditary postmaster general, also made the Rothschild sons his Court-Agents. More titles were obtained from impecunious sovereigns in return for small loans. The Grand Master of the Order of St John was in financial trouble after the expropriation of his properties in France. He appointed Amschel as his Court-Agent and was granted a personal loan of 200,000 gulden, a sum still not repaid long after it was due many years later. The rulers of two other petty principalities, the Count of Isenburg-Birstein and the Duke of Aschaffenburg also appointed Amschel as their Court-Agent. In this case, the appointment, at least, guaranteed Amschel the supply, annually, to his door, of "72 hundred-weights of hay, 72 of oats, 10 cartloads of straw and 30 cords of beech wood".*

* * *

---

* When, in 1814, Aschaffenburg was annexed by Bavaria, Amschel asked for reconfirmation of these deliveries in view of his services to Aschaffenburg, "at a time when [its] public purse was completely exhausted . . . and no one else would have granted it [a loan]. Nor has the money until this moment been repaid". Under the circum-

What mattered more now than hollow titles was experience, access to capital markets and a feel for the changing political scene. Money was short everywhere. Napoleon's military campaigns were turning large parts of Europe into theaters of war, while his bitter struggle with England had left its imprint on all the continent's economies. Germany was particularly struck by the scarcity of credit. As bankers and major importers of English goods, the fortunes of Rothschild and his sons were directly affected by these changes. Trade with England and the international capital market were their main concerns.

Nathan was establishing a thriving branch of the family business in England. After a few months of apprenticeship with Levi Barent Cohen, his father's banker in London, he had settled in Manchester. England was a milder, more benign climate for Jews, and Nathan enjoyed a freedom there not found anywhere on the continent. There were no ghettos and public humiliations. Indeed, the Jewish boxer Daniel Mendoza and wrestler Abraham da Costa were national idols.

Voltaire's famous description of the London Stock Exchange comes to mind:

> Go into the London Exchange, a place more dignified than many a royal court. There you will find representatives of every nation quietly assembled to promote human welfare. There the Jew, the Mahometan and the Christian deal with each other as though they were all of the same religion. They call no man Infidel unless he be bankrupt.

Voltaire would never have written these lines about Frankfurt. Nathan was almost immediately successful. His father insisted that he stay in touch with the parent firm every post-day. The letters show that they regularly exchanged business, political and personal news. Rothschild could be furious when Nathan was tardy in his replies.

As it was, Nathan had much to report. England was the world's

---

stances, Amschel argued in 1814, "the payment in kind should be seen as deserved compensation of our loss". Negotiations about the straw, the hay and the oats continued until 1817 when the wealth of the House of Rothschild already amounted to several million pounds sterling.

leading center of banking and credit. Manchester was the center of the English textile industry, which had recently been mechanized. Nathan was amazed to discover that prices were sometimes a fraction of what they were in Germany. Large armies were gathering everywhere on the continent which had to be clothed and the demand for all kinds of cloth was constantly rising.

Nathan threw himself into the challenge with the fervour of youth and with considerable talent. Contemporaries describe a stocky, bright-eyed young man with a shock of red hair and a reputation for a prodigious memory, who exuded an impression of overflowing energy. He had brought with him to England a tradition of buying with cash when the market was low and of selling in volume at rising levels of profit. His initial capital of £20,000 was considerable. Yet within a short time he had doubled and then tripled it. With so much capital he had become a young merchant-prince, set apart from the struggling Jewish shopkeepers in whose company he attended synagogue services in Manchester. He conformed "strictly to all the rites and ceremonies . . . his [kosher] dinner being cooked by a Jewess [was] taken to his warehouse every day". Within a few years, a sizeable part of the city's trade with the continent was in Nathan's hands.

Back in Frankfurt, Mayer Amschel Rothschild was forwarding or selling Nathan's shipments of English goods at heretofore unheard-of high prices. Nathan was his father's agent, using his seal (MAR) until at least 1809. He supplied his father's needs in textiles and in colonial goods – indigo, tea, dried fruit, sugar and coffee. But he quickly built up a business of his own; he had a growing list of clients in France, Sweden, Switzerland and even Russia. By 1802, Nathan was borrowing money in London on his own account. In 1805 he opened an office there. In 1806 he married Levi Barent Cohen's daughter Hannah, whom he had met in her father's house during his first days in England, when she was still a teenager. The bride's dowry was £10,000. Her father was said to be the richest Jew in England, the hub of a kinship network that linked the Goldsmids, Mocattas, Montefiores and other important Jewish financiers in the City.

Rothschild was pleased with his son's marriage, enthusiasm and success. Yet as a critical and strict father, he also anguished over

Nathan's casualness and disorganized work habits. He would be furious if he suspected that Nathan was keeping something from him, as these extracts from his letters show:

> Dear son, a father who has to think of the happiness of all of his children must be excused if he wants to know the real state of your fortune. If you have a number of bad debtors . . .

> My dear Nathan, you must not be angry with your father; unfortunately you are not very good in writing. You should engage . . . a secretary.

He sometimes felt that Nathan neglected his duties towards his partners. Nathan might announce the arrival of twenty-seven bales of cloth but send only twenty-six; or write to his father saying that he was sending a case bearing this or that number which, when it arrived, bore a completely different one. And his book-keeping was untidy:

> If, then, you are so disorderly – especially as you have no friend, nobody to help you – you will be the victim of thieves all round . . . lack of order would make a beggar out of a millionaire . . .

Then, this piece of reminiscence:

> In my youth I was, just as you are now, a very active merchant, but there was no order in my business. The reason was that I was a student in Talmud, I had learned nothing of practical business life. You have brains but you did not learn to keep order . . .

Some of Rothschild's business letters to Nathan were written by secretaries in English. Nathan's own English was still halting. His clerks complained that it was impossible to ascertain from his letters what he really meant. The personal exchanges between father and son were in *Judendeutsch*, the patois of the Frankfurt Jews, which they wrote in beautiful, large, cursive Hebrew letters. Rothschild reported proudly:

> Our Jacob is already working in our comptoir, and he only just became bar-mitzvah

Caroline, Salomon's young bride, wrote to Nathan to congratulate him on his success, wishing he would build "a big warehouse [in Manchester] and a bridge over the Seine [in Paris]", while Guttle fretted over his health and wardrobe:

> Dear son Nathan,
>   I sent you with Kassel and Reiss 6 shirts and with Ezriel Reiss also 6 shirts, 2 scarves and with Michael Bing you will get 2 tablecloths. If you tell me the length and width I shall send you more. I have some on the bleaching ground. Be well and wear the shirts in good health.
>   Guttle, wife of the honoured Meyer Rothschild

She shunned all waste. In 1801, while Calmann was visiting Nathan in Manchester, to learn English in preparation for joining the family firm, she wrote:

> I want to remind my dear Calmann to bring me what lies around in Nathan's house, from [unclear] to all sorts of other things he does not need, whatever it is, because I can use everything here, also tableware and something pretty for my dress. I shall remain forever your faithful mother.
>   Guttle, wife of Meyer Rothschild

In Frankfurt, Rothschild was converting a trading house and a medium-sized discount and exchange shop into a major banking concern. As he gained access to substantial new funds, thanks to Buderus and to Nathan's success in England, he made first attempts to negotiate state loans.

In the beginning he was content to do so in partnership with established Frankfurt banks, but not for long. In Kassel, a power struggle was taking place between Buderus, who supported Rothschild, and another war counsellor, Kaspar Harnier, who patronized his son's banking firm of Ruppel & Harnier. The two were surreptitiously breaking open each other's sealed letters. The Landgrave was aware of their rivalry and may even have encouraged it in order to extract better terms for himself. Rectitude, in the modern sense of this term, was neither practised nor expected in the eighteenth

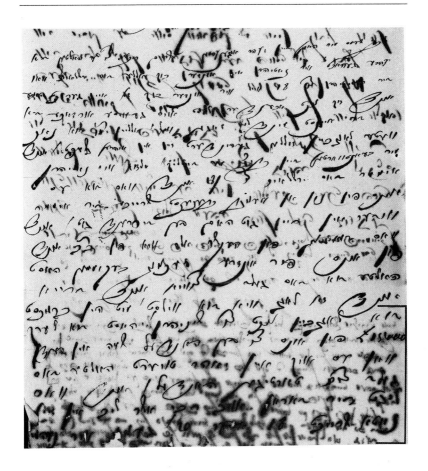

Part of a business letter to Nathan Rothschild in London written in
Judendeutsch (German in Hebrew letters) by his brothers in Frankfurt.
The postscript (marked) is by Mayer Amschel. Most letters from
Rothschild to his sons and between the sons were in this script.
(*Courtesy N. M. Rothschild Archives, London.*)

century. As long as everyone behaved gracefully and caused no dam-
age to the Landgrave, the conflicting personal interests of highly
placed civil servants were taken for granted. Senior officials were
willing recipients of gifts euphemistically described as "douceurs"
(sweetners). A great Roman theologian lent his tacit support to this
practice, saying that he found nothing wrong with officials accepting
gifts provided they undertook nothing contrary to their prince's
interests.

Even though Buderus's monthly salary was only eighty gulden, his "douceurs" had accumulated over the years to make him a relatively rich man.* Additionally, his private investments, thanks partly to Rothschild, were yielding a nice profit. His great aim, according to his great-grandson, was to leave his six children a nobleman's title as well as an independent income. For this reason he had recently purchased a nobleman's estate outside Hanau and formally applied to the Austrian Emperor to grant him a knighthood. He was, in his way, a decent, hard-working man.

By helping Rothschild to gain access to the Landgrave's funds, Buderus was enabling him to negotiate large loans to foreign governments at little risk to himself. The Landgrave had large surpluses and was ready to buy up large packets of foreign state bonds much in the same way that pension funds today acquire shares and treasury bonds. As an institutional broker, Rothschild's function was to match the Landgrave with the right borrower. He negotiated prices, rates of interest and dates of maturity. Wilhelm's capital continued to grow and he was eager to invest it. At a time of acute money shortages, the profit on medium-term loans could be as high as 20 per cent.

Josef Sauer, the economic historian of the Landgraves of Hesse, defined Wilhelm as "a pure capitalist" for whom the making of more and more money had become an obsessive end in itself. He was systematically withdrawing revenues from the state's coffers and investing them abroad for his own profit. At the same time, he was pressured by cousins and in-laws in several European royal families to lend them money at lowered rates of interest. For this reason he tried his best to be thought poor, not rich, and preferred, whenever possible, to lend money anonymously, through trusted intermediaries.

There were also political reasons for lending anonymously. The grant or refusal of a loan to a foreign power was almost always a political act with political consequences that the Landgrave wished to avoid. For political reasons, he was, of course, moved from time

---

* "Who could blame him?", his great-grandson, Lother Buderus von Carlhausen, wrote in a biographical essay on his ancestor a century later. "Men of higher birth and rank, whom I do not have to name, used the same means [to get rich] and still use them to this day."

Wilhelm IX, Landgrave of Hesse. Oil painting, artist and date unknown. From a private collection, London. (*Courtesy N. M. Rothschild Archives, London.*)

to time openly to lend money to powers such as Prussia or Austria but, as a general rule, he preferred lending only to states weaker than his own. He believed in the old Latin saying *Noli fenerari fortiori te, quod si foenerveris, quasi perditum habe* – Money lent to those stronger than you is practically lost.

It was Rothschild, apparently, who first suggested that the recently introduced *Partialobligationen* (partial bonds) would best safeguard the anonymity the Landgrave desired. Partial bonds were a clever new financial device: offered in small denominations to the public at large, and quoted on the stock market, they enabled wealthy rulers like Wilhelm to lend their money anonymously by buying up these bonds through reliable intermediaries. They were negotiable and payable to the bearer. Wilhelm's poverty-stricken Danish in-laws never need know where the money they would borrow against partial bonds came from.

How cautious Rothschild still was, as he made his first steps in this field, can be seen by the limited share he assumed in one of the first loans he offered the Danish court on this basis, early in October 1800. He negotiated the loan but assumed responsibility for only one-sixth of the total amount. Two other banks handled the rest. The entire package of 4 per cent Danish partial bonds was sold, at the usual discount, to the Landgrave. In due course, Rothschild collected and delivered the interest payments. His profit at this time was still relatively modest, consisting mostly of commissions. But from then on, Rothschild's growing affair with "the richest man in Europe" never stopped. Commissions tended to multiply. There were commissions on signature and upon delivery and maturation, when interest coupons became due, when turned into cash and when exchanged into local or foreign currency. Bonds were normally offered below value, say at 70 per cent of nominal value, and were redeemed at the full price; the ensuing profits to the Landgrave and to Rothschild would be considerable.

The first sale of Danish and other partial bonds to the Landgrave was handled jointly by a syndicate composed of Rothschild and two Frankfurt banks. In late 1801 and early 1802, the sales become larger. We now find Rothschild in Kassel negotiating these larger sales alone. To cover his needs he was himself borrowing large amounts of money from the Landgrave: 320,000 gulden at 4 per cent in 1801; another 200,000 gulden seven months later. The Landgrave was strict in his requirements for collateral; Rothschild had to deposit treasury notes with him to the same value.

Between 1801 and 1806, Rothschild negotiated eleven loans adding up to 5,000,000 gulden, mostly to Denmark and Darmstadt-

Hesse. To further mask the origin of the moneys, another intermediary was interposed, a Hamburg banker named J. D. Lawaetz. Lawaetz was in close contact with the Danish court, and a personal friend of Buderus. Copenhagen was in contact with Lawaetz in Hamburg, Lawaetz with Rothschild in Frankfurt, Rothschild with Buderus in Kassel, and vice versa. Lawaetz assured the court in Copenhagen that the lender was "a very rich [Frankfurt] capitalist, exceptionally friendly to the Danish Court. It is possible that even greater sums and better conditions can be obtained from him". Nor was Rothschild uncomfortable in his role as the anonymous lender, hiding behind Lawaetz. The competition among bankers in Frankfurt and Kassel over state loans financed with the Landgrave's millions was strong. Buderus was slowly easing out Bethmann Brothers, Ruppel & Harnier and Moses Joseph. All were smarting from their defeats. Rothschild was careful not to antagonize them further. He was linked to Bethmann and Ruppel & Harnier in a series of other syndicates, joint loans to the cities of Frankfurt (400,000 gulden), Hanover (650,000 gulden) and to the Duke of Mannheim (500,000 gulden). How ably Rothschild managed to keep his competitors in the dark can be seen by the fact that in November 1805, Bethmann Brothers and others were still making offers to Denmark on deals that already had been concluded with Rothschild, through Lawaetz, more than eight months earlier. Bethmann's, who had first introduced partial bonds into the German market, was an old conservative bank. In contrast, Rothschild's was the new, enterprising house.

Heine, the great German romantic poet, made fun of both Frankfurt houses: "Haven't Rothschilds and Bethmanns long been *at par*? Businessmen all over the world have the same religion. Their comptoir is their church". But they were not at par. Bethmann's bank was in trouble even without Rothschild's aggressive competition. It had not reckoned sufficiently with the recent political upheavals. "At this time of the greatest money shortage", Christian Wilhelm Berghoeffer, with access to papers that are now lost, wrote in 1922, "Rothschild appeared more resourceful and more efficient than the banking house which occupied the prime position not only in Frankfurt but throughout Germany."

*   *   *

These affairs, and others, required Rothschild to travel constantly. He was hardly back from Munich, in connection with some property deal, when he set out for Hamburg to meet Lawaetz. In either direction it was a trip of a week or more on rough roads. Post-coaches were often nothing but long covered wagons with two hard benches on either side, and neither straps nor strings. In bad weather they travelled at walking pace and often overturned on the muddy roads. Travellers had to spend the night at nearly every station. The postillions would stop at every tavern to down a pot of beer. Travellers had to put up with this or bribe them to go on.

Lawaetz's attitude to Rothschild was at first rather reserved. Before meeting him he wrote to Buderus: "Herr Rothschild always struck me as unusually solid, prompt and fully worthy of confidence. Yet some caution is called for, since we are dealing with a single individual and a significant sum of money". After meeting Rothschild in person, he wrote to Buderus: "People who dislike our good Rothschild promise us that Bethmann's loan [of 500,000] will cost less and be quicker arranged than Rothschild's . . . [I will] support the good Rothschild as well as I can . . . Envy may speak against him, but he is a good man who deserves respect." In the event, Bethmann's cheaper offer never materialized; unlike Rothschild, Bethmann was unable to fulfil his promises.

So much travel took its toll. Rothschild's health was failing. He suffered mysterious bouts of tiredness and fever, and from a bad case of hemorrhoids.* In 1801, the Frankfurt senate invited Rothschild to assume the post of *Baumeister* (titular head of the Jewish ghetto), a position of considerable power and responsibility. The post was usually offered to one of the richest or most learned men in the Judengasse. Since Rothschild was as yet neither, the offer reflected his growing prominence, perhaps as head of the Jewish welfare board. Rothschild declined the offer on account of his deteriorating health.

---

* Hemorrhoids were a common complaint in the ghetto. "The lower classes in the Judengasse (who run around all day) are generally in good health", S. Behrends, author of a book on health, fertility and mortality in eighteenth-century Frankfurt, wrote in 1798. "The grander Jews of business, however, often spend the entire day in the musty street. They are sickly . . . as are the learned Jews who sit forever over the Talmud. One result of this way of life is that nowhere are so many people tortured by hemorrhoids as in the Judengasse."

He submitted medical certificates to substantiate it which declared: "The sitting position is detrimental to his health".

While other bankers mostly awaited orders to reach them in their *comptoirs*, Rothschild went out to solicit them. In 1801, he regularly stayed in Kassel, where Buderus lived, for weeks at a time, often with Amschel or Salomon accompanying him. They were in fact establishing a second branch office. This brought protests from his oldest competitors, the court-Jews of Kassel, Moses Joseph and Feidel David. They complained that he was a "protected Jew" of Frankfurt, not of Kassel, and therefore had no right to do business in their city. Not only was he stealing their business but he was not liable for the special tax that out-of-town Jews were obliged to pay for each night they stayed in Kassel.

In August 1803 Rothschild petitioned the Landgrave to recognize him and one of his sons as "protected Jews" of Kassel. He explained that their considerable financial interests in northern Germany necessitated their prolonged stays in Kassel. He was, in fact, asking for permanent residence permits. Their presence in Kassel, he maintained, would in no way harm the city of Kassel; on the contrary, he wrote (shrewdly appealing to the Landgrave's interests), the resulting competition would be in the public good.

The Kassel revenue officer was of a different mind. He recommended that Rothschild's request be rejected since it ran counter to the Landgrave's own rule that the number of Jews in the city be kept at a minimum. But since Rothschild was, as he put it, "a very rich Jew", the revenue officer referred the final decision to the Landgrave himself. The Landgrave was attracted by the possibility of more competition among bankers seeking a slice of his business. The record states that "Meyer Amschel" (sic) be recognized as a "protected Jew", provided he ran only a bank in Kassel and donated 400 reichsthaler toward the construction of the new "Neustadter church".

Rothschild made the required donation. He then had second thoughts. He had been warned that if he took out residence in Kassel he might be taxed twice, in Kassel as well as in Frankfurt. The matter was left pending for almost two years. Rothschild and his sons continued their affairs in Kassel as intensively as before. There were further protests. Rothschild was again asked to declare himself. He had another change of heart. In his unlettered German he wrote:

> Serene Prince Elector
>
> Most Gracious Prince and Lord!
>
> Your Princely Highness has most graciously deigned to allow the granting of protection for me or my son and I have long ago made payment of the 400 rt due for this purpose: My son now desires to join his brother in London, I am resolved therefore to assume the protection myself and humbly beg Your Princely Grace to deign order that the letter-of protection be issued in my own name.
>
> At the same time, I offer to pay the local Jewish community the customary public tributes, and in addition to that as much as Moses Joseph pays, who, as is well known, is one of the richest protected Jews here, on condition that I will not be publicly assessed, for I am not permanently present here, and do not gain all my means only here . . .
>
> I remain in the deepest submission
>
> Your gracious Prince's humblest servant
>
> Meyer Amschel Rothschild.
>
> Kassel, the 8th July 1805

Once again the revenue officer rejected his request. He may have been in the pay of Rothschild's rivals. The revenue office informed Rothschild that he would be granted "protection" in Kassel only if he actually moved his family, his *comptoir* and his entire property there.

This Rothschild refused to do. It was not easy to live or work in Frankfurt; but Frankfurt was the center of a life that he would not leave. The family was growing. In 1802, Rothschild's second daughter Belche had married Bernard Sichel, the son of a wool merchant in the Judengasse. In January 1803, Salomon's wife Caroline had given birth to a son, Rothschild's fourth grandchild. Every two years or so, Nathan came over from England to visit.

The house itself at the "Green Shield", where he lived with Guttle and the remaining children, was more comfortable now, more private, even cosy, with new rugs and utensils that Nathan was sending over from England. The rooms were no longer as cluttered with the bales of cloth, sacks of coffee and goods the Rothschilds traded in. But the Judengasse was still bleak and musty. Most of the burnt-out ruins had not yet been rebuilt after the fire of 1796. Many of the remaining houses looked "more like stables, more like thieves' dens than human habitations", one Christian visitor wrote in 1807. "How sombre and dark is this lane, how black and sooty most of the houses look", wrote another, adding, "Our Jews are for the most part experienced businessmen. I don't think I exaggerate when I aver that without the Jews our city would not be as flourishing and important as it is now".

Some of the major and most of the minor oppressions were still in force. The senate continued to remind all Jews who had settled in the Christian city after the fire that their sojourn there was strictly temporary; it made ready to force them back into a restored, somewhat enlarged ghetto. The humiliating *Stättigkeit* (Jews' Statute) was still read out publicly every year in the synagogue. The post office withheld letters addressed to Frankfurt Jews until the afternoon to allow them to be censored; the recipients were able, however, to see the envelopes. Rothschild "arranged that letters which contained information about the state of the market would be sent in colored envelopes . . . if the pound rose – blue, or fell – red". Thus, "half a day is saved", Rothschild explained.

To accommodate the growing volume of his imports from England, Rothschild had a few years earlier, as we have seen, been able to rent storage space close to the Judengasse in the Christian city. As usual, since the lessee was a Jew, the lease was subject to strict limitations. The premises had to be inaccessible directly from the street. They could not be identifiable as business premises or shops by written signs or other markings. In October 1803, the magistrate informed Rothschild that he was violating a decree of 1748 that confined Jewish warehouses to the ghetto. He was ordered to vacate his new premises on the Schnurgasse or face charges. Rothschild's son Amschel assured the magistrate that no signs were hung nor were goods ever displayed outside, but his plea was rejected. However it is not clear from the municipal record whether the order was ever enforced.

On the other hand, it was now possible for Jews to leave the Judengasse on Sundays, although on a "temporary" basis only, and on payment of a tax. The old prohibition against Jews entering public parks was also beginning to break down, albeit partially. This was the result of an international incident. One day in 1804, a French Jew named Cohn was roughly handled by militiamen for entering a public park. The French commandant Fouquet immediately pressed for damages. *"C'est une satisfaction que je demande pour la nation française!"* The militiamen were arrested and ordered to apologize to Cohn. An official announcement in the *Journal de Francfort* gave the apology a public character. Because of the "difficulty in distinguishing" between local and foreign Jews, reported the paper, the prohibition could no longer be enforced.

The dire circumstances of the Jews of Frankfurt were becoming a *cause célèbre* in revolutionary France. The Paris papers criticized the Frankfurt senate for maintaining a "medieval ghetto" and demanded the extension of full civil rights to the city's Jews, while non-Jewish bankers and guilds voiced their concern over these "crude interventions" in Frankfurt's domestic affairs. Rothschild's main competitor, Simon Moritz von Bethmann, went so far as to warn that if the Jews were granted equal rights the ordinary people of Frankfurt would have to emigrate since they would be deprived of their daily bread. The senate's permanent emissary in Paris, a man named Abel, protested that the condition of Jews in Frankfurt was an internal matter and not the business of any Frenchman. The recurrent criticism had an impact, however. Abel himself urged the senate to allow a greater number of Jews to move from the Judengasse to healthier homes outside.

Educational facilities in the Judengasse remained backward. They had hardly changed since the early Middle Ages. For this Jews had to blame only themselves. "The slightest reform is anathemized here", a writer in *Sulamith*, the local Jewish family magazine, complained. A few of the richer families were able somehow to enroll their children in schools outside the ghetto, including the famous humanistic *Gymnasium* of Frankfurt. The poor and the obstinate continued to attend the old *heder*. Rothschild had been aware of the latter's limitations for a long time. A chance encounter, in the fall

View of the Judengasse, 1895. The synagogue is on the left. Aquarell by
C. T. Reiffenstein, date unknown. (*Courtesy Historical Museum, Frankfurt.*)

of 1803, gave him an opportunity to help change the existing system.
On a visit to Marburg, he happened upon a little wandering Jewish
orphan from Galicia who earned himself a meagre living by singing
Hebrew songs at street corners and inns. Rothschild was so taken by
the boy he brought him back to Frankfurt, and asked Geisenheimer
whether something might be done for him.

He knew that Geisenheimer had long been planning to establish a modern Jewish school. A few weeks after the orphan's arrival, Geisenheimer and three other young men, with Rothschild's help, formed an association to found a new school "for poor children of the Jewish Nation", to be called "Philantropin". Its aim was to spread "the love of mankind" and educate young Jews in the spirit of Pestalozzi (the great Swiss educational reformer) and the enlightenment. It would teach the Torah as well as the ideas of Voltaire, Rousseau, Lessing, Herder and Moses Mendelssohn.

Rothschild's young orphan was among the first three boys to be enrolled in the new school. Its first premises were still inside the prescribed area of the enlarged ghetto. Rothschild's bookkeeper, Geisenheimer, was on the new school's board of directors. Jacob Rothschild's tutor, Michael Hess, was head teacher. In addition to traditional, sacred studies, German, French, geography, natural history and modern philosophy were also taught. Its guiding principle was "Torah and Derekh-Eretz" (torah and customs of the land); students were exhorted to be "a Jew at home and a Mensch [human being] outside". The Judengasse was sharply split over the new school. For its readiness to pursue secular studies, the new school was bitterly attacked by the orthodox rabbinical establishment. The Frankfurt magistrate had to restrain the Chief Rabbi from formally banning it. Christian opinion on the new school was also divided. "The hatred seems to increase with the spread of enlightenment among Jews", a writer in *Sulamith* claimed. "It seems as though the Christian gentlemen begrudge Jews the light of knowledge and are downright eager to keep them in their ignorance." Rothschild was orthodox, but he must have sensed the inadequacies of his own education throughout his life; he knew that in addition to traditional subjects, a modern education, such as the one Hess had given his youngest son Jacob, was now a necessity. He supported the new school. His eldest son Amschel continued to support it financially throughout his life.

CHAPTER FIVE

Forging the Dynasty

IN AUGUST 1806, WAR again broke out between Prussia and France. Throughout spring and early summer, Wilhelm, the Landgrave of Hesse, had negotiated with both sides in the hope of attaching himself to the party offering him the greatest gain. He leased 20,000 Hessian soldiers to the Prussian King, against payment of £250,000. At the same time, he made overtures to Napoleon and promised to remain neutral in exchange for the rich city of Frankfurt and its southern territories. The Prussians offered Wilhelm the prospect of becoming King of Hesse, a rank that he had lusted after for years.

The negotiations dragged on with threats and promises on all sides. Wilhelm's chance to reach an accommodation with Napoleon evaporated in July, when he refused to join sixteen other German states that were uniting under French tutelage in the Confederation of the Rhine. Napoleon's patience finally ran out in October. After winning a decisive victory at Jena, Napoleon ordered his troops to march on Kassel, some one hundred miles to the west. His generals were to arrest Wilhelm and confiscate his treasures. He "is practically a Prussian, if not an Englishman, and sells his subjects' blood for money . . . The House of Hesse will cease to reign . . . Its existence on the banks of the Rhine is irreconcilable with the security of France".

Wilhelm received the bad news in the middle of the night, at Schloss Wilhelmshöhe in Kassel. He had just finished refurbishing it at enormous cost. "At twelve at night I am awakened; I was so terrified I expected an apoplectic stroke", he noted in his diary. "I rose immediately. With Buderus I was able to put many things aside"; that is to say he arranged hiding places for some of his dearest *objets*.

There was no question of opposing the French advance. Nor was he under any illusion that his last pathetic attempt at survival, the posting of signs on the main access routes to Kassel saying *PAYS NEUTRE*, would deter the French troops from occupying his lands.

Wilhelm's main concern was for his own safety and that of his treasures and investments, both at home and abroad. A detailed plan, drafted a few weeks earlier, for just such a contingency, was put into action. It listed all that was to be evacuated and all that was to be hidden, and where.

Buderus was at the Landgrave's side at all times. Invoices and account books from the past twenty to thirty years were carefully sifted. Everything that indicated the whereabouts and extent of the Landgrave's investments, his annuities, deposits and loans at home and abroad was sorted and packed to be hidden or sent away. A growing band of valets and aides was at work day and night at the palace packing suitcases and crates. Gold and silver plates and trinkets, family jewels, candelabras, snuff boxes and gobelins, his collection of rare coins and medals (many of which Rothschild had supplied), were packed in boxes; also piles of business papers, deeds of trust, loan contracts, title deeds, treasury notes, bonds and other sureties. As an added precaution, the coupons for collecting interest payments were detached from the bonds and concealed separately.

The Landgrave at first intended to ship a number of crates containing his best silver by river to Bremen and from there to England. But his negotiations with the boat's captain broke down over a matter of fifty thaler. He ordered the silver to be hidden with the rest. Altogether, 119 crates were secreted behind false walls at the palace, and in the two picturesque castles of Löwenburg and Sababurg. The first French troops reached the outskirts of Kassel on 31 October 1806. That same night, the Landgrave escaped the city disguised in civilian clothes. He was accompanied only by his eldest son, his English account books and a few lackeys. The party, in two coaches, each pulled by six horses, drove unrecognized through the French lines straight to the Danish frontier and, with little ready cash, reached its first destination, the estate of Wilhelm's brother Karl at Gottdorf, outside the city of Schleswig.

In Frankfurt, Rothschild followed these events with growing trepidation, perhaps even panic. Buderus had confided in him for years. Few outsiders had as clear an insight into the Landgrave's vast and varied fortune as he. In addition to his own self-interest, Rothschild felt a certain loyalty to the prince who had granted him a measure of protection and respect thirty-five years earlier. He may have been happier if his patron had reckoned better with Napoleon's forceful character. During the past five years, he had gained a lead over his competitors for the Landgrave's enormous business; all this was now at risk.

Amschel was in Kassel. He must have reported the Landgrave's downfall in gloomy terms. There was no way of knowing how much of his fortune the Landgrave had succeeded in salvaging before his precipitous escape.

Buderus had remained behind to handle last minute arrangements. He followed his master the next day, leaving his distraught family behind. He took the same route, not by coach-and-six but on foot, disguised as a wandering craftsman, with a leather knapsack on his back filled with coupons detached from Danish or English bonds. Near the castle of Sababurg, Buderus stopped briefly to hire a peasant's cart and was shocked to discover that the Landgrave's secret hiding place had become public knowledge. Everywhere people were talking of the treasures "hidden" in the castle.

The French military Governor-General, Lagrange, lost no time looking for them. In Sababurg he found a great hoard of gold and silver, which he ordered to be melted down, and the Landgrave's coin collection, which he sent to Paris to be auctioned. A small army of French-appointed clerks scanned the remaining accounts in an effort to locate the Landgrave's main debtors. The latter were to be offered substantial reductions if they settled with the French commissioners instead of with the deposed landgrave. By December, Lagrange had uncovered the location of nearly all the remaining crates. The more treasures he found, the more eager he was to feather his own nest. In return for a bribe of 1,000,000 francs, he was ready to fabricate the accounts and report to Napoleon that only treasures worth around 16,000,000 gulden had been recovered; the remaining 22,000,000 in bonds, bills, cash vouchers and mortgage documents could then be smuggled out of the country.

The legend of "The prince gave my father his money". Two paintings by
Moritz Oppenheim commissioned by Rothschild's sons after the Napoleonic
wars. In the first, the Landgrave entrusts Rothschild with his treasures. The
second shows the restitution of the treasures, presumably with compound
interest. Oil paintings, Moritz Daniel Oppenheim, 1861, from a private
collection, London. (*Courtesy N. M. Rothschild Archives, London.*)

The Landgrave's representatives were more than willing to enter
this scheme. Lagrange kept his side of the bargain. The retrieved
crates were dispatched to the Landgrave in Denmark or deposited
in safe houses in Frankfurt. Rothschild agreed to hide four crates in
the secret cellar under his house in the Judengasse. This later gave
birth to the persistent legend that the Landgrave, in a melodramatic
scene prior to his exile, had placed his millions in Rothschild's faithful
hands. Rothschild was said to have hidden these millions in wine
barrels under his house and to have handed them back after the war
with compound interest.

Rothschild's sons themselves nurtured this legend after the war

as a public relations device. Calmann approved without comment its diffusion in Germany's leading encyclopedia. Amschel commissioned two "historical" paintings depicting the mythical scene from a well-known Frankfurt artist. Nathan, in an after-dinner speech in 1834 claimed;

> The prince gave my father his money; there was no time to be lost; he sent it to me. I had 600,000 pounds arrive unexpectedly by the post; and I put it to such good use that the prince [after the war] made me a present of all his wine and his linen.

The truth was less melodramatic. The suspicious Landgrave would never, of course, have entrusted *all* his money to one man. The four crates deposited in Rothschild's cellar contained only some old debentures and bonds without their coupons. But it is true that in exile, Wilhelm gradually gave Rothschild access to his salvaged fortune. By 1809, Rothschild would be its main, if not only, administrator. Despite Rothschild's earlier fears, the Landgrave's exile would prove to be a stroke of extraordinary luck.

During his first days at Gottdorf in Danish Schleswig-Holstein, the Landgrave was gloomily brooding over his fate. Napoleon's troops were unpleasantly close, only some fifty miles away in Hamburg and Wilhelm lived in constant fear of being kidnapped. The arrival of Buderus cheered him a bit.

"Buderus, thank God, with Me", he noted in his diary. "He gets the appointment of Secret War Counsellor from Me and adopts the name of von Carlshausen." He also decided to more than double Buderus's monthly salary from eighty to 168 gulden. But the faithful Buderus refused to accept the raise. He did not "want to be a burden", he wrote.

Without many of his account books and cut off from his main debtors, the Landgrave had little choice but to entrust the administration of his finances to Buderus. As a first step he gave him power of attorney to collect the interest due from debtors in England and Austria. Buderus assigned these tasks to Rothschild. He advised the Landgrave that at such a time as this, his fortune was best administered from a single point through an able and discreet man like Rothschild. The versatile Rothschild was better able to handle it than some petrified old banking house.

There was no way of telling how much was salvaged or lost. Buderus suspected the worst. A week after his arrival in Gottdorf, he wrote to Lorentz, the Landgrave's agent in London: "We are in the greatest misery here. Please help us to get some money soon because we do not know what we shall do otherwise, as we are not getting a farthing from Kassel. God, how things have changed."

Wilhelm's only completely safe funds were those invested in London under false names, at an average interest of 3½ per cent. Their nominal value was £860,000. The Landgrave wondered how, in view of his reduced circumstances, the income on these funds could be raised. Then, gradually, things calmed down. The situation cleared. News of Lagrange's corruptibility arrived. The Landgrave was now better able to calculate his apparent losses. They amounted to a total of 21,000,000 gulden. But with 30,000,000 gulden still in his possession, Wilhelm remained one of the richest capitalists in Europe. He and Buderus settled down to administer the remaining fortune and if possible to augment it. Rothschild's immediate task was provide the means to cover Wilhelm's personal and political needs. These included his day-to-day maintenance and the support of his dependants – his numerous offspring, his spouse who had not followed him into exile and his current mistress, the Countess von Schlottenheim, who had. Rothschild also forwarded Lagrange's bribe.

The Landgrave's English bills continued to arrive in Frankfurt at a steady flow. Rothschild continued to discount them. He also collected interest payments on a recent loan of 1,500,000 gulden to the Austrian Emperor. Other big debtors were contacted directly by Buderus. French offers of discounts were countered by the Landgrave with tempting offers of his own, accompanied by warnings that the French occupation could not last.

Wilhelm had not become less miserly or more trusting of his entourage in exile. Buderus bore the brunt of his squeamish moods. With patience, elaborate displays of humility and with a fine psychological sense, Buderus urged Wilhelm to do things his way, through Rothschild and his sons. Rothschild wrote to the Landgrave directly, offering his services. In the first letter, written in his usual broken German (for which, however, he had no need to feel self-conscious since the Landgrave's own syntax was only a shade better than his), Rothschild assured Wilhelm of his loyalty, even to his last drop of blood.

The Landgrave brooded over the alternatives. In December he presented Buderus with a written questionnaire. The central question was No. 14. Was it really possible, he asked, "to trust Rothschild and would he, or Ruppel & Harnier, allow themselves to be used by [Napoleon's] investigation commission?" Buderus answered unequivocally:

> Rothschild has on all occasions to date displayed the most loyal attachment to Your Serene Highness. He, as little as Ruppel & Harnier, will not allow himself to be used by the investigation commission, unless they have to give way to violence.

Only Rothschild's "most loyal attachment" is being attested here by Buderus, not that of Ruppel & Harnier. A few days later, Buderus returned to French-occupied Germany to coordinate Wilhelm's remaining business interests, which under the circumstances was an act of courage, as well as extraordinary loyalty. He passed briefly through Kassel to collect his wife and children. With his family he retired to his new estate outside Hanau, in the French zone of occupation but only an hour's ride from Rothschild's *comptoir* in Frankfurt.

Rothschild's long-standing alliance with Buderus revealed itself now as a masterpiece of business administration. Buderus's town house in Hanau became the clandestine center. Rothschild, nearby in Frankfurt, was his executive arm. At a time of acute money shortages everywhere and much depreciation in the value of paper money, Rothschild's bank was suddenly able to dispose of relatively large funds. The Landgrave's annual surpluses at this time – after the deduction of all his personal and political expenses – were about 700,000 gulden. The funds he deposited with Rothschild after 1807 may have been more than 1,000,000 gulden annually. Rothschild's capital grew rapidly and his bank rose to become a major, though not yet the major, house in Frankfurt.

Buderus kept the books and negotiated with the debtors. Rothschild was responsible for collecting payments. Both were in touch with leaders of the patriotic underground working for the Landgrave's return. The patriots were rebelling against the oppressions of foreign French rule but were ready, as patriots often are, to submit again to the local tyrant. Buderus's house was full of secret drawers and other hiding places. He coordinated all money transfers to the Landgrave and reinvested the surpluses, which were still growing all the time. He was under constant surveillance by the French police who suspected that he was working for the exiled Landgrave. For this reason he kept only his coded account books at home, never coupons, money or other incriminating documents. Promissory notes, debentures or coupons he received from Denmark he immediately transferred to Rothschild, who redeemed them. All payments were deposited in the Landgrave's current account at Rothschild's bank and reinvested by him according to instructions issued by

Wilhelm's questionnaire and Buderus's answer (No. 14): "Rothschild has on all occasions to date displayed the most loyal attachment to Your Serene Highness." Hessische Hausstiftung Schloss Fasanerie Eichenzell bei Fulda. (*Courtesy Jewish Museum, Frankfurt.*)

Buderus. The arrangement was profitable for Rothschild and convenient for Buderus, whose house the French police periodically searched for proofs of the Landgrave's financial transactions.

For his own protection, Rothschild kept two sets of books. One set was for the French authorities, the second was hidden in the secret cellar under the house. The French continued their investigations, but not very thoroughly and their silent connivance could often be bought. Moreover, they were dependent on members of the local administration of Frankfurt, some of whom were German patriots. The prevailing sentiment in Frankfurt and Hanau – among Christians as among Jews – was of solidarity against the foreign invader. In the summer of 1807, French agents offered Rothschild a cut of 25 per cent on any of the Landgrave's English annuities he might be willing to surrender. He solemnly denied he had any. The French inspectors examined his books but found nothing incriminating.

One of Rothschild's sons, usually the young Calmann, was now almost constantly on the road on the Landgrave's business. He was the Landgrave's and Buderus's main courier, collecting the interest and the capital payments on the Landgrave's local loans and travelling between Frankfurt, Hanau and Denmark. Rothschild had a special chaise, with a built-in secret compartment, constructed for this purpose by a carriage-maker in Hanau, a confidant of Buderus. Political messages were also conveyed by this means. But its main purpose was to enable Calmann to travel safely, picking up coupons, delivering bonds, collecting moneys and depositing them. He also supplied some of the Landgrave's other requests, and those of his growing entourage – jars of seltzer water from Hanau, honey, once a cork-screw and even a pair of Dutch clogs.

Rothschild's "official" balance sheet for 12 May 1807 shows that his assets on that day totalled 1,973,192 gulden. It is one of two that have survived. Between 1797 – the date of the earlier balance sheet – and 1807, his official assets had more than quadrupled. In the spring of 1807 he established a temporary branch-office in Hamburg. Its main purpose was to enable him to be nearer to the Landgrave and to give Calmann a local base. The Landgrave was feeling safer now. He had bought a house at Itzehoe on Danish territory, not far from Hamburg. Rothschild installed himself in Hamburg for weeks at a time and drove out to visit the Landgrave at Itzehoe. The two men discussed the Landgrave's investments and took long walks in the Landgrave's park.

Despite this unprecedented intimacy, the Landgrave was still not completely reconciled to the fact that all other bankers had been dropped or were used only very rarely. He was not sorry about Ruppel & Harnier, whom he suspected of wrong-doing. But he was unwilling to give up the services of the renowned old Frankfurt banking house, Bethmann Brothers. It was one of Germany's largest and impressed Wilhelm with its great wealth and aristocratic reserve; he scolded Buderus for squeezing them out. But Buderus insisted that he had done the right thing and, in August 1807, there were angry exchanges between them on this subject. The Landgrave also wanted Buderus to live nearer to him, in Hamburg or Schleswig-Holstein. Buderus refused to budge from Hanau.

Early in September, Wilhelm summarily ordered Buderus to present himself at Itzehoe to finally resolve their differences on this matter. Buderus arrived in a sombre mood. Overbearing and fussy, Wilhelm chastised him for working almost exclusively with Rothschild. Flustered, Buderus protested his absolute devotion to his master and insisted that Rothschild was offering the best service under the circumstances, and the best terms. Try as they might, his competitors never bettered him; none were ready to take the risks and work as hard. The Landgrave's business was not an ordinary business; Rothschild and his sons were ideally suited to handle it. They were efficient, discreet and courageous. They took serious risks. Bethmann, on the other hand, was over-cautious and biding his time. Since the Landgrave had gone into exile, Bethmann had been avoiding him, Buderus complained, whereas Rothschild proved his loyalty and concern daily. Moreover, in recent months Bethmann seemed to have exhausted his resources.

Buderus insisted that working with Rothschild was in the Landgrave's best interest. And he bitterly complained that the Landgrave was being unfair to him. "Your Grace has no idea of my work burden. I have no secretary and must write everything myself . . . my day begins at 4 in the morning and is often not over by 10 at night."

The meeting ended inconclusively. Back in his room that same night, Buderus feared that he had not made his case as well as he should have. He sat down and wrote the Landgrave an impassioned, almost threatening, letter. There was "no difference whatsoever between a gulden from Rothschild and a gulden from Bethmann", he wrote. But it was a fact that Rothschild always offered better terms. He was fair, punctual in his payments and above all shrewd in keeping everything secret from the prying French, who had tempted him in vain with fat commissions. They had been unable to find anything incriminating in his books. Two days later Buderus wrote again: "Deadly to an honest man is so much distrust", and offered his resignation. This last thrust had the desired effect. The question of Rothschild or Bethmann was never again raised. Nor did Bethmann Brothers make an effort to regain what they had lost. The Rothschilds were undoubtedly surpassing them in both vigor and imagination.

While all these events were taking place, the political situation in Frankfurt was changing. The Holy Roman Empire of the German Nation, which had been moribund for years, finally perished in the fall of 1806. Frankfurt's ancient status as a "Free Imperial City" came to an end; with it also ended the humiliating status of Frankfurt's Jews as "serfs of the chamber". The city was incorporated into the new French-dominated Confederation of the Rhine. Karl von Dalberg, the Prince-Bishop of Mainz who had collaborated with Napoleon in its creation, was the new sovereign of the city and the surrounding territory.

Dalberg's appointment was a fact of some importance to the deposed Landgrave and to Rothschild. A former high official of the defunct Holy Roman Empire, Dalberg had changed sides and joined in creating the new Confederation of the Rhine as a third German force to offset the weighty power of Austria and Prussia. As a Catholic, Dalberg was wary of Prussian militarism; at the same time, he was not Napoleon's stooge. He was well disposed towards the Landgrave and he seems to have had some business dealings with Rothschild in the past.

Dalberg was a man of the Enlightenment; religiously tolerant, he was a friend of Goethe, Schiller, Herder and the Humboldt brothers. He arrived in Frankfurt in September 1806 and immediately confirmed his reputation as a liberal by ordering *all* parks and promenades in the city opened to Jews. The Jews of Frankfurt, who had fought for this privilege for over a century, welcomed him as their saviour, declaring he was the "Prince of Princes! The Beloved of God!"

But while, in his first decree, Dalberg readily granted members of all other religious groups – Lutherans, Catholics and Calvinists – the right to serve in public office, "the Jewish nation" was only promised "protection against insults and libelous outrage". Christians were merely enjoined "to meet Jewry in a spirit of humane benevolence".

Rothschild did his best to ingratiate himself with the new lord of Frankfurt. Dalberg was aware that he and Buderus continued to serve the Landgrave in secret, but saw little wrong in that and even warmly commended Rothschild to the French generals and ministers. At Rothschild's urgings, he intervened to protect Buderus from undue harassment by the French.

In the same letter to the Landgrave (15 December 1806) in which he pledged his undying loyalty, Rothschild passed on a message from Dalberg, who wished Wilhelm to know that he had interceded on his behalf with Napoleon and promised to do so again on the Emperor's forthcoming visit to Frankfurt. At the same time, Rothschild reported, Dalberg was advising the Landgrave to be less contentious and instead approach Napoleon as a humble petitioner.

Rothschild was useful to Dalberg in other ways too. Like other satraps of Napoleon at that time, Dalberg was in constant need of cash. His civil list amounted annually to 350,000 gulden. It covered salaries, pensions and the precious political and diplomatic gifts common at the time, which Dalberg distributed freely to his courtiers and to visiting dignitaries. The old patrician banking houses of Frankfurt refused Dalberg's frequent requests for loans; Rothschild, in contrast, granted them readily. In return, he urged Dalberg not to delay granting the Jews of Frankfurt full civic equality. Dalberg was ready to make Rothschild a full citizen immediately, before any decisions were taken about other Jews. Rothschild declined his offer.

He "did not consider himself worthier than his co-religionists. For this reason he refused to be given priority."

In July 1807, Napoleon paid a state visit to Frankfurt amidst much talk of civic freedom and reform. The Judengasse celebrated his arrival with a triumphal arch. A delegation of Jewish dignitaries welcomed him at the city's gate. In an "Ode to Napoleon the Great", recited in German, French and Hebrew, the Emperor of the French was hailed for raising "the remnant of Israel from the dust and lending it his mighty arm". Nevertheless, little, if anything was done to remove the remaining disabilities. Jews still paid the special tax and were banned from entering coffee houses or walking through the main city squares. In the public baths, towels were still marked "for Christians only". Rothschild's second son, Salomon, was denied permission to move out of the ghetto (where he had been living with his wife's parents since 1800) and rent an apartment in the Christian city. Amschel, Rothschild's eldest son was also still living with his wife in his father's house, twelve years after their wedding, since there were no vacancies in the Judengasse. The publication of a weekly magazine in Hebrew or *Judendeutsch* was refused permission as it might become a means for the diffusion of "Jewish obscurantism".

The combined forces of commercial rivalry and religious prejudice were still powerful enough to delay the full emancipation of the former "serfs of the chamber". Dalberg lacked determination and strength of will. Faced with so much opposition in the city to his plans for reform, he vacillated. In the end he decided to issue a "improved" Jews' Statute, to supplant that of 1616.

The new statute, issued on 4 January 1808, came as a bitter shock to most Jews. Rothschild must have felt betrayed. Unlike the new liberal constitutions of Westphalia that, under Napoleon's brother Jerome, conferred full equality on all Jews, Dalberg's new statute for Frankfurt continued to treat them as a foreign body. The radical writer Ludwig Boerne lamented the "inexplicable horror" inspired by Jews which "like the ghost of a murdered mother continues to accompany Christianity".

The new statute revived most of the discriminating restrictions of the *Stättigkeit* of 1616. It obliged Jews to vacate the rented homes in the Christian city where they had been living since the fire of 1796;

they were to move back, within a set period of time, into a rebuilt and enlarged ghetto. It made them collectively punishable for misdemeanors and debts, reimposed the old poll tax, set the maximum number of Jewish families in the city at 500, limited the number of marriages to twelve in any given year and excluded Jews from key trades and professions as before. As a concession to the new liberal spirit, when taking an oath they would no longer have to repeat the offensive formula "if I break this oath I will suffer all the penalties and .maledictions which God imposed on the cursed Jews". Instead they would only invoke "the penalties and maledictions which God imposed on those Jews who rebelled against him in the desert and were cursed for this". Boerne remarked sarcastically: "What loyal citizen, free of rebellious lusts, would still harbor resentment at having to repeat this vow?" If the law of 1697 had allowed only six shops in the Judengasse, the new statute granted them between four and six more. It made civic equality in the future entirely dependent on the "unanimous, explicit and formal agreement" of the Christian citizenry.

The new statute in some ways was harsher than the old. All rabbinical appointments would henceforth require confirmation by the Lutheran consistory. Circumcisions were to be performed only with permission of the government.

Protestations against the new statute were to little avail. Goethe, who maintained that Jews, like women, had no "point d'honneur", defended Dalberg. He was not to be faulted "for treating this race as it is and as it will remain for some time". The spirited Bettina von Arnim, later a famous romantic writer, took Dalberg to task for his new statute. Dalberg defended himself lamely, saying that he "was not indifferent to the misery of the Jews; there was a question, however, of whether they would not *misuse* their freedom. Wouldn't they balance Christian injustice, as soon as they breathed some air, with Jewish impudence?"

"They can't be worse than their oppressors", Bettina retorted, but Dalberg was not moved. He remained for most of the year at Napoleon's court in Paris. A deputation of Jewish notables from Frankfurt visited him there to protest at the new statute. Rothschild helped to defray its cost. Dalberg continued to vacillate.

*   *   *

Less than a month after the Landgrave had given Rothschild access to his money, Napoleon provided him with a golden opportunity to put it to profitable use. In the Edict of Berlin, issued on 21 November 1806, Napoleon announced the closure of all continental ports to English goods. "No ship which comes directly from England or her colonies shall enter any of our harbors." All trade with England was prohibited. Violators were threatened with confiscation of their goods as contraband merchandise. Austria, Prussia, Sweden, Denmark and Russia were requested to join the blockade.

Napoleon had not reckoned sufficiently with the ingenuity of the Frankfurt merchants, from the staid Bethmann Brothers and Rothschild down to the last cotton and wool peddler. All threw themselves with gusto into trade in contraband English goods and all made a good deal of money. It was also the "patriotic" thing to do. Frankfurt had always been the central market-place for English and colonial goods for much of the European continent, including even large parts of France.

The new nationalism combined with the old profit motive to make Frankfurt the center of continental efforts to break the French embargo on English goods. The English government offered smugglers special premiums for undermining Napoleon's scheme. "The trade in English and colonial goods never flourished in Frankfurt so much as it did after the imposition of the French blockade." Rothschild and his sons played a major part in the orchestration of this boom. A fleet of cargo ships was at Nathan's disposal to transport goods to ports on the Dutch and north-German coast. His brothers were in attendance at all ports of call to forward the merchandise on to Frankfurt and other destinations on the continent. The brothers spread out to take care of all details. Calmann was in Hamburg, Salomon in Dunkirk and Jacob in Amsterdam, where Amschel also seems to have spent nine months in 1808 in connection with this business. An elaborate messenger service linked the brothers with London and with the "Green Shield" in Frankfurt. Rothschild coordinated everything. French attempts to stop them were half-hearted or ineffective.

Early in the crisis, M. J. Bing, one of the Rothschilds' worried clients in Frankfurt, wrote to Nathan in Manchester:

4 November 1806

I want only to remind you to take all possible precaution with forwarding the goods which I have ordered with you, because in my opinion there was never before such a dangerous time for forwarding English manufacture to the Continent as now ... the emperor of the French will take possession of the Hanse towns. Therefore I advise you to keep the goods with you until further notice.

His concerns were unfounded. Ten months later, Rothschild triumphantly informed Nathan:

20 August 1807

You can't have any idea how [English] goods are demanded in our markets now. I sold all the cambrics left to me from 3 years ago ... try if you can send by Holland. That's the best speculation to be made.

The public buring of contraband English goods by French troops in Frankfurt, November 1810. The value of burnt goods was estimated at 1,200,000 francs. Anonymous engraving. (*Courtesy Historical Museum, Frankfurt.*)

There were the usual exchanges of political news between Rothschild and his sons:

> *8 July 1807*
> Emperor Alexander and Napoleon were together at Tilsit and peace is no doubt with both . . . I hope that we will have soon a general peace

> *21 March 1808*
> It seems that Sweden will have to make peace with France and Russia and then our transactions with Sweden and [?] will be ruined.

And the usual complaints about Nathan's disorderliness, by the same Mr Bing:

> *16 June 1807*
> You always send messages by your father and that is very disagreeable. Can't you keep up a regular correspondence with me in a businesslike way, or will you give up business?

Rothschild's activities on behalf of the exiled Landgrave were continuing as before. Wilhelm's great coin and medal collection had been put up for auction in Paris and at Wilhelm's request Rothschild was able to buy large parts of it back. Afterwards, Buderus had to remonstrate with his master for "poor Rothschild to be finally reimbursed" for the moneys he had laid out. He asked one of the Landgrave's courtiers to reflect on where they would all be if it had not been for Rothschild's devoted services.

In 1808, the Landgrave, for reasons that are not clear, urgently needed several hundred thousand gulden and turned to Rothschild for a loan. Rothschild begged off; too much of his capital was now invested in (English) merchandise, he told the Landgrave. But he did supply the Landgrave's estranged wife with the money she needed; he also paid out pensions to those of Wilhelm's former court officials who refused to collaborate with the French and to Hessian officers detained as war prisoners. Such payments could not have been made clandestinely.

In the spring and early summer of 1808 he again installed himself in Hamburg on a near-permanent basis. The Landgrave still lived nearby at Itzehoe. Rothschild found him in an anxious mood. His presence there was becoming an embarrassment for the Danish royal house and he was preparing to depart again. He gave Rothschild a few chests full of deeds, debentures and other valuables for safe keeping. A few days later, on 20 July, the Landgrave departed, in great haste, travelling unrecognized through French-occupied territory to Prague, where he had been offered asylum by Francis I, the Austrian Emperor.

Rothschild's long journey back on the rough roads was more gruelling than the trip out had been. He arrived back in Frankfurt late in July and immediately fell seriously ill. "A wound in one of the most sensitive parts of the human body" was said to be the cause of a "dangerous disease". It may have been diabetes. The standard medical procedure at the time for all diseases was to regularly bleed the patient to the point almost of collapse. The family feared for his life. On 30 July 1808 he made his Will. Professor Ledig, a surgeon from Mainz performed "a risky but successful operation". He remained confined to his bed for several months.

On 30 August, at the instigation of Dumeniel, the French Commissaire-Imperial, he was suddenly summoned by the Frankfurt magistrate to a hearing on the Landgrave's finances. Rothschild was bedridden, so Salomon was allowed to appear in his place. Salomon arrived at the magistrate's with some trepidation, for General Lagrange's double-dealing had recently come to light and Buderus had also been arrested. The French undoubtedly knew by now the extent of the Rothschilds' involvement in the Landgrave's affairs, but the questions put to Salomon were so bland and considerate to a point where one suspects that someone, perhaps Dalberg himself, had intervened in their favour. The interrogation was brief. The court record, usually so detailed, covers less than one page. Salomon had to answer a few general questions on his father's business relations with Buderus. He testified that Buderus had invested a small sum of money in his father's firm. The investigator wished to know if Buderus was communicating with them by registered or by normal mail. Salomon said that he did not remember. No more questions were asked. Salomon was ordered to relay to the police all future communications from Buderus, and was dismissed.

The Landgrave was now in Prague with an entourage of thirty-six attendants that included Rothschild's eldest son Amschel. Wilhelm, who had been a good-looking young prince in his youth, was now in his sixties, bent and obese and suffering from gout. His features were permanently distorted by mysterious swellings in his face. He had recently bought a fine palace in the city and an estate in the country. The transaction had been handled by Amschel Rothschild, who travelled back and forth between Frankfurt and Prague.

Wilhelm's archive had followed him to Prague from Itzehoe and Hanau. The Austrians, angling for his money, treated him with the honors due to a foreign potentate. Rothschild senior was too weak to travel himself to Prague; instead he corresponded with Wilhelm and his courtiers. Codes and cover addresses were used, to mislead the French and Austrian censors. Rothschild signed his letters to Prague as "Peter Arnoldi"; the Landgrave was "Goldstein", Buderus "Wahlschmid". Nathan's codename was "Langbein". Pounds sterling were "rabbi Moses", while the code for English Consolidated Stocks was "Jerusalems". The Landgrave asked Rothschild for the chest full of valuable papers he had left with him as he fled Denmark in July, which had still not arrived. Wilhelm was beside himself with worry, recording his growing concern over this chest in his diary. He noted Amschel's periodic arrivals, always without the chest. On Christmas Eve 1808, Wilhelm panicked and perhaps suspected the worst. On Christmas Day, finally, his mood improved: "At 3 p.m. the youngest Rothschild arrived with all the important papers of coffre No. 3. God be thanked for this!" The delay may have been caused by Rothschild's illness or his fear of intensified French surveillance.

This "youngest" Rothschild was the sixteen-year-old Jacob. When he or Calmann were not in Amsterdam or Hamburg receiving one of Nathan's illicit shipments, they too were rushing back and forth between Frankfurt, Hanau and Prague, carrying messages and money, and on occasion filling Wilhelm's special requests – a jar of Frankfurt mustard, a bottle of oil or some eau de Cologne. Calmann brought Wilhelm the news of Buderus's recent arrest which, naturally, threw the Landgrave into deep concern. Nathan wrote to ask that Calmann settle in London to assist him. Amschel wrote back to say that Calmann was needed elsewhere for "the main business". The "main business" was the continuing effort of the Rothschilds to make more of the Landgrave's funds in England available to Nathan, which Wilhelm had not yet fully authorized.

Rothschild's secret partner: Karl Buderus von Carlshausen. The only surviving picture is this silhouette of a handsome man at a small table writing or administering his accounts. Silhouette based on a lost original, *c.* 1811. (*Courtesy Jewish Museum, Frankfurt.*)

The brothers' extensive involvement with the distinguished exile in Prague naturally aroused the curiosity of the Austrian government. The Austrian chief of police in Prague was asked to report on it and on 12 March 1809 informed Vienna that "under the cloak of business" the Rothschilds were conducting important political activities on behalf of the exiled Landgrave. Whenever he entered the Landgrave's palace, the Austrian chief of police reported, he always found Amschel there, in the company of Wilhelm's highest courtiers.

One of Rothschild's letters to the exiled Landgrave in Prague, smuggled through the French lines and signed by him with the codename "Peter Arnold", 1809. (*Courtesy Jewish Museum, Frankfurt.*)

"They go into their own rooms and Rotschild [sic] generally carries papers with him."

Amschel shuttled between Prague and Vienna. As Imperial Crown-Agent he had some standing in Austria. He was one of the Landgrave's intermediaries in his negotiations with the Austrian treasury. The Austrian Emperor wanted money for his campaign against

France. Amschel and his father advised the Landgrave to delay. Instead of lending the Emperor more money, they suggested, the Landgrave might transfer some of his outstanding claims against individual debtors. The Emperor of Austria might be more successful than the exiled Landgrave in bringing his debtors to book. The Landgrave liked the idea. He sent the Emperor a long list of outstanding claims amounting to more than 10,000,000 gulden. The Emperor, understandably, was unwilling to serve as the Landgrave's debt-collector. The scheme was abandoned but it gave the Rothschilds a first opportunity to negotiate directly with an emperor who within a few years would grant them titles of nobility.

Calmann or Jacob was Wilhelm's connecting link to Buderus. He also passed along messages between Wilhelm and patriotic rebels in Hesse planning insurrections against French rule. In one such message, carried to Prague in the secret compartment of Calmann's carriage, an anonymous rebel informed Wilhelm that:

> there will be no shortage of people ready and willing to sacrifice everything . . . [if they] could be certain of receiving the necessary financial support.

As an added safety measure, Rothschild had transcribed this message into Hebrew script. After safely arriving with it in Prague, Calmann retranscribed it into German.

This was dangerous work. Hesse was now part of the new kingdom of Westphalia. The new king, Napoleon's brother Jerome, lived in Wilhelm's former palace in Kassel. The rebels were planning to abduct him from there and seize power. The plot did not mature, perhaps because Wilhelm would finance it only *after* its successful conclusion, and not a moment before. But Wilhelm's role in the simmering rebellion was public knowledge. The French made a new effort to crush it. On 8 May 1809, Buderus was again arrested. His house in Hanau was searched. Nothing incriminating was found but his family was molested. His sister was roughly interrogated with a loaded pistol pointed at her head. Buderus was transported to Mainz prison like a common criminal. He continued to proclaim his innocence. He was merely a retired gentleman, he claimed, and was released on bail.

147

The investigation now turned once more in the direction of Rothschild. It was headed by the Westphalian chief of police, a tough French commissaire named Savagner, who pursued it with skill and determination. Savagner suspected, not unjustly, that Rothschild was administering the exiled Landgrave's fortune and that he had been the channel through which the recent uprising in Westphalia had been financed. But he lacked proof. In Hanau, which was in Westphalian territory, Savagner had been free to act as he saw fit against Buderus. In Frankfurt, he was in Dalberg's semi-independent realm. Dalberg refused to sanction Rothschild's arrest. Under pressure from King Jerome's ambassador, Dalberg gave in but insisted that Savagner's warrant be "extremely limited".

Rothschild was warned in time to prepare himself for Savagner's visit. Everything that could be remotely compromising was removed from the house. Even the secret cellar was cleaned out. The four crates filled with the Landgrave's account books and other valuables were moved through the underground passage to the cellar of a neighboring house.

On 10 May 1808, two days after Buderus' arrest, Savagner arrived at the "Green Shield". A detachment of constables took up positions in and outside the house. Nothing like this had been seen in the Judengasse for a long time. Rothschild and his two sons, Salomon and Jacob, were placed under house arrest. (Amschel and Calmann were absent, Amschel was in Prague staying with the Landgrave, and Calmann was on the Danish coast forwarding on Nathan's shipments from England.) Rothschild was confined to his bedroom. A police constable was posted at the door. Salomon and Jacob were kept under guard downstairs in the *comptoir*. All cupboards and chests containing papers were sealed. The house was systematically searched from the attic down to the pump-room on the ground floor. Dalberg's own police chief, von Itzstein, was present throughout to make sure Savagner did not exceed his mandate.

Limited as it was, Savagner's mandate was broad enough to give Rothschild a difficult enough time for nearly a week. On the first day he endured a rough interrogation that lasted several hours. The surviving protocol shows that Savagner was fairly well informed but lacked concrete proof. The search did not provide any. Rothschild's wife, Guttle, and their daughters and daughters-in-law were also questioned. They had been drilled to stick to an agreed version. They were not in contact with the deposed Landgrave; they had absolutely nothing to do with the failed uprising; Buderus was only a minor, occasional, private client.

Savagner came prepared with a set of questions which he pressed relentlessly on Rothschild and other members of the family. Rothschild's answers were not always cogent. The record clerk must have been half asleep or else Rothschild was deliberately incoherent. In response to a question about his age he replied "approximately sixty-seven years". He rambled. Savagner scolded him for giving "completely confused answers". The old man pleaded sickness and fatigue. He claimed he had lost a good deal of his memory as a result of the operation he had undergone in the previous year.

Savagner questioned him closely on his family and on his business. Where were his other sons? Rothschild answered vaguely that Nathan was living in England and had married, he did not know exactly when, maybe eight or ten years ago, perhaps less; Calmann was in Copenhagen and Amschel in Vienna or Prague, but was expected back at any moment now. He denied that Amschel had gone to Prague to help the Landgrave in his financial speculations. Savagner found this difficult to believe. Rothschild insisted that he was there in connection with a lawsuit against a Bohemian nobleman.

To protect his sons, Rothschild claimed that he alone owned the business. His sons owned no part in it, they were merely his aides. And he was Buderus's banker, he claimed, not his friend. All transactions on behalf of Buderus were registered in his books.

Savagner seems to have been briefed on the details of Rothschild's affairs by one of his embittered competitors in Kassel, a man named Levi. He knew of Rothschild's stay in Hamburg during the summer of 1807. Hadn't he opened an exchange-shop there together with Buderus? Rothschild insisted that he had been to Hamburg in connection with a shipment mistakenly branded as contraband from England. The mistake had been cleared up and the merchandise released. He had also engaged in some banking business there, but certainly not with Buderus. Any friendship he may have shown Buderus was "only for the eyes of the world, not *innerlich* [inwardly]".

Had he not crossed into Denmark and met the Landgrave at Itzehoe? Had he not spent hours with him in his rooms and walking in the garden? Yes, Rothschild confessed brightly, but this was only natural since he had been the Landgrave's court-agent for almost forty years. He had negotiated some loans for him in the past but no longer remembered the details.

Rothschild constantly pleaded fatigue and asked to be excused. He was still confined to his bedroom. In the *comptoir*, Salomon and Eva were showing Savagner through the account books. Rothschild was brought in again. Since Amschel was now in Prague, was not it fair to assume that he was making illegal deals with the demoted Landgrave? If Amschel was doing so, Rothschild said, it would be without his knowledge.

So it went. The interrogations and house searches continued for nearly an entire week. The house was turned upside down. Savagner went home in the evening. The constables stayed on. Nobody was allowed to enter or leave. Rothschild and his sons remained under house arrest. Salomon's house was also searched. Salomon said as little as possible. Why had his brother Amschel gone to Vienna? He was an Imperial Crown-Agent, Salomon said. It was once a very honorable title in Frankfurt, he added sardonically, even though this was no longer so. Late at night he was allowed to go home for a few hours of sleep. He had been kept in the *comptoir* under police surveillance for days. Jacob claimed he was only a young apprentice and knew little of what went on. He had never heard that his father gave financial support to the rebels. Rothschild's daughters and daughters-in-law claimed they were only "office machines", they had seen Buderus once or twice but did not know who he was. Guttle refused to answer any questions saying only that she was busy all day with the household and knew nothing of any business.

Rothschild was interrogated again and was warned once more to speak only the truth. He reiterated that because of his illness and age he no longer remembered many details. He referred his interrogators to his account books. The investigators carefully went over them. They unearthed many details but remained ignorant of the context. They discovered the records of payments Rothschild had made to one of the Landgrave's consorts. This was serious, but apparently not serious enough to warrant criminal procedures. Other than this, nothing positively incriminating was found. The investigators never found the concealed door leading into the secret cellar. However, French police reports on the matter show that they were not fooled. The French police commissioner of Mainz reported to Paris that "Rothschild had been warned ahead of time by the Frankfurt police". There was no doubt in his mind that Rothschild was keeping "a double set of books". The problem was that none was found. Perhaps Savagner had been purposely negligent in looking for it, for even as he was searching the house he demanded and received a bribe of 3,000 gulden. (This helped to bring the investigation to an earlier end.)

Six days after their arrest, Rothschild and his sons were released with a warning not to have any further dealings with Buderus without informing the authorities. Rothschild immediately wrote to Savagner's superiors in the government of Westphalia that his arrest had been unfair and had damaged his reputation. At the very least he demanded a formal declaration that the investigation "had not raised the slightest suspicion or mistrust".

This was done. Rothschild could breathe more freely. But the experience served as a warning to steer a more cautious course between the exiled Landgrave and the new masters of Frankfurt. Henceforth, the Rothschilds would no longer limit themselves to the service of a single sovereign. With Nathan in London and, he hoped, another son in Paris in the near future also, the Rothschilds would establish themselves as a European, today one would say as a "multinational", bank. When the Landgrave, a short time after this, asked that Rothschild, or one of his sons, take up permanent residence in Prague and become part of his immediate retinue, Rothschild declined. Only a short time before, this would have been a highly flattering offer. Now he begged permission to refuse it for reasons of health and overwork. Buderus seconded him: "The father is an old sick man", he wrote to the Landgrave. "His oldest son [Amschel] and his second son [Salomon], whose health is also delicate, are indispensable to him in his extensive operations. The third son [Calmann] is travelling on behalf of Your Grace almost without interruption, the fourth [Nathan] is established very profitably in London and the youngest [Jacob] is staying with him there."

In his search through Rothschild's files, Savagner failed to discover that three months earlier, on 17 February 1809, Buderus had formally become a silent partner in Rothschild's firm. In a "binding agreement" – and an investment of 20,000 gulden – he committed himself "to advise the banking firm of Mayer Amschel Rothschild as best he can in all business matters and advance its interests as far as he may find feasible". In return he was granted access to the accounts. He now had an added personal interest to promote Rothschild's business.

Immediately after this, Buderus finally won the Landgrave's consent to appoint Nathan Rothschild as manager of his English funds. The Landgrave's surpluses in England were growing all the time. It was no longer feasible to transfer them to Prague. What had finally won over the Landgrave was the fact that Nathan was content with a commission of only 1/3 per cent as against ½ per cent charged by the London bank – van Notten & Co. – that had handled these surpluses for generations.

Nathan began by investing the Landgrave's surplus funds in English Consolidated Stocks of a nominal value of £150,000. Paying 73 per cent of face value, the Landgrave felt he was getting a bargain. Even before the capital was fully paid, he ordered Nathan to invest another £150,000 on the same terms. The stocks were purchased in Nathan's name since some of the Landgrave's other English funds had recently been sequestered by the government. It is easy to imagine how this fact alone vastly increased Nathan's credit standing in the City of London. In September 1810, Nathan was asked to acquire a third batch of £250,000. The total, then, was £550,000. The credit standing of one with stock worth £550,000, registered in his own name, would have been very considerable. Nathan made good use of it. To possess nearly unlimited credit during an acute cash shortage, as this was, was tantamount to a licence to print money.

It was the biggest and most profitable transaction between Rothschild and Wilhelm of Hesse to date. One recalls again Nathan's claim, often dismissed as light-hearted after-dinner banter: "The

Landgrave gave my father his money ... I had £600,000 arrive unexpectedly by the post". Of course, the money did not arrive in the post; and the figure he gave was imprecise. The story may have been an attempt to veil the true sequence of events. The successful administration of these £550,000 may well have been the basis for Nathan's subsequent meteoric rise in the English financial world. Calmann confirmed this six years after the event in a letter to Amschel:

> Nathan ... writes again about the Landgrave.
>
> The Landgrave made our fortune. If Nathan had not had the Landgrave's £300,000 in hand, he would never have got anywhere.

The first big profit came with Nathan's purchase of stocks at a lower rate. The second came when he sold them at a higher. The third, and biggest, was made when Wilhelm began paying in installments. The market in English stocks was so constructed that in the interim, between receiving the funds and investing them, the Rothschilds were able to make profitable use of them on a short term basis. Wilhelm often complained about these interim periods. Buderus assured him that his previous bankers, van Notten, had also held on to funds for months at a time and "had never paid a single gulden in interest." Nevertheless, Buderus reassured the Landgrave, Rothschild was ready to pay a modest rate of interest.

With Wilhelm's money Nathan was able to make the first grand speculations for which he would later become famous. (At that time, Nathan was very profitably speculating in gold bullion.) Wilhelm suspected that Nathan was manipulating his money but the Continental Blockade impaired communications between Prague and London and left Nathan with plenty of opportunity to manoeuvre with funds whose origins had to remain secret.

The trade with English goods, despite Napoleon's attempts to scuttle it, also continued. The value of Nathan's monthly exports to Frankfurt in 1810 averaged £20,000. They rose to more than double this amount during the summer months. His father master-minded and financed much of this operation from Frankfurt. The premium on English goods during the continental blockade is said to have been 50 per cent and the Rothschilds' profits from this source alone may have been more than £100,000 annually. Nathan became a naturalized English citizen in 1804. His mother Guttle kept sending him cakes and shirts. He was now permanently installed in his new "Counting House", at 2 New Court, St Swithin's Lane, near the Bank of England. Upon moving into his new place he requested the post office to deliver his mail henceforth by special messenger rather than by the regular post. Time was money. Nathan was almost too quick for his prudent, conservative father. It was the source of some contention between the two. With the ablest of his five sons, Rothschild was stern, impatient and sometimes even severe. One begins to understand why there had not been enough space for them all in Frankfurt, and why Nathan had felt he must get out:

M. A. Rothschild, Franckfurt to N. M. Rothschild, London:
28 June 1809
I beg not to be troubled in future with similar confusion and countermand . . . I have not such a large personnel . . . Moreoer, I repeat once and for all that your writing in "Hebrew" is allright for family matters but in order to make yourself understood on accounting and business matters you must ensure that you use German, French or English script and language, since I cannot present my accounting staff with your Jewish script and its underlineations interspersed with family news if they are to keep good books – and a good deal of confusion arises.
Franckfurt 15 November 1809
. . . and now my dear son I can't help but show you my surprise at your behavior against me and your family by keeping secret the purpose and end of your journey . . . it is your duty both toward a friend-parent and as an associate to act openly and give us every post-day true relations of the way and kind of your affairs. I understand . . . you want some money. I forward you this remittance of £4705 5s 6d . . . I pray you at this moment to write me very great and clear letters and believe me I always remain
Your loving father Mayer Amschel Rothschild.

And yet the Rothschilds were already too dispersed, their affairs too widespread and varied to be directed exclusively from the center by one man. On 27 September 1810, Rothschild and his elder sons drew up a new "irrevokable" partnership agreement. In the old agreement of 1796, Amschel, Salomon and Nathan had been junior partners in a firm directed exclusively by their father. The new partnership agreement redefined these roles and established a new, delicate balance between the "chief" and his grown-up sons. The sons were authorized to commit the firm and given the right of signature. The new deed stimulated their industry by granting them more substantial shares in the business's profits. It paid homage to their father's "proven industry, good business sense and experience, who through his tireless activity from youth to advanced age, was the sole cause for the present flourishing state of the business and the worldly happiness of his children". For this reason he retained the "decisive vote" as "chief" of a business to be directed, however, by all partners. Rothschild reserved to himself the right to withdraw funds at his pleasure; his partners agreed not to undertake any business, or withdraw money without the prior knowledge of the others.

The partnership contract assessed the capital value of the business at 800,000 gulden. The father's share was 370,000. Amschel and Salomon were each allotted 185,000. Calmann was allotted 30,000. Profits and losses were to be computed in proportion to these shares; at a future date, presumably after Mayer Amschel's death, his five sons could divide the business between them in equal parts. As a minor, Jacob could not yet join the firm as a "real partner". The contract assured him his share upon his coming of age. Until his twenty-first birthday, he was allotted a capital of 30,000 in the firm, duly earned through his "conscientious execution of business tasks" entrusted to him in the past. Interestingly, the contract alluded also to losses, "mortgages, debentures, and bills of which unfortunately! much is no longer realizable and has turned bad ... or is likely to turn bad".

The absence of Nathan's name in this document is noteworthy. He was not, however, disinherited by the old man. On the contrary, Nathan was on the best of terms with his family. Amschel was four years older than Nathan but recognized his superior ability. He

A signed copy of the partnership announcement (1810) between Rothschild
and his sons. The charred remains were found in the Fahrgasse after the sack
and destruction of the Rothschild Museum by the Nazis in 1938.
(*Courtesy Jewish Museum, Frankfurt.*)

deferred to Nathan, calling him "our dear and wise teacher".
Nathan's name was left out of the official document because, as an
English citizen living in enemy territory, it was deemed politically
wise at the time. His father was holding Nathan's 185,000 gulden

share for him. There was a secret, subsidiary agreement, to this effect. The agreement was signed only by three sons but was valid for all five.

The document throws a fascinating light on Rothschild's evolving dynastic scheme. The line of succession would be strictly limited to male offspring. Wives, daughters and their children would not inherit the firm and had no right to inspect the company's books. The partners and their heirs were enjoined "not to molest [sic!] the company with litigation". Heavy penalties were foreseen for breaking this rule. In the old man's lifetime, he was to be the sole arbiter between his sons. After his death, all differences had to be submitted to neutral arbiters appointed by the parties; their decision was final and not subject to appeal. Not all of these terms may have been enforceable under the law, but they reflected an overriding desire to perpetuate unity among the brothers, prevent the dispersion of capital and retain, as far as possible, the compact, disciplined, well co-ordinated character of the family firm.

To mark the transition the name of the firm was changed to "Mayer Amschel Rothschild & Sons". A printed letter went out two days later to all clients and friends:

> The active assistance, which my sons A. M., S. M., and C. M. Rothschild have rendered me for many years moves me to accept them as real partners in my business firm . . . which, as I flatter myself, I have been running for more than 40 years to the satisfaction of my friends.
>
> As I express my vivid thanks for the confidence shown to me until now, I would ask you to extend it also on my associates and be assured that we will have no more earnest desire than to honestly serve our friends and deserve their continuing confidence.
>
> Yours faithfully
> Mayer Amschel Rothschild
> whose signature will be
> A. M. Rothschild will sign
> S. M. Rothschild will sign
> C. M. Rothschild will sign

CHAPTER SIX

Towards Emancipation

Rothschild's pace now slackened. Overall control remained in his hands, but most of the burden was carried by his five energetic sons. At sixty-seven, infirm, often ailing, Rothschild was able at last to repose. He took English lessons. An inner tension seemed to have relaxed.

There was little rest, however, in the efforts to gain full civil rights. These still lagged far behind. The discriminating Jews' Statute was still valid. Even when not fully enforced, its strictures remained as humiliating as before. Residents of the old Judengasse, including Rothschild, were still prevented from moving to healthier parts of the city. Those who, since the fire of 1796, had been living in rented homes in the Christian city were threatened with criminal charges unless they moved back into the ghetto by specific dates. For the first time in his life Rothschild accepted public office. As a leading member of the new *Vorstand* (executive) of five notables from the Judengasse, he reminded Dalberg of his past solemn promises.

The weak-willed Dalberg continued to waver. He had recently received his share of the booty which Napoleon had bestowed upon his satraps after the defeat of Austria at Wagram. It consisted of additional territory and a nice new title. He was now Grand-Duke of Frankfurt, with an expanded realm modelled after a French *departement*. On civil rights he was still reluctant to defy majority opinion. On 19 October 1810, he said publicly that full equality for Jews would be "highly dangerous", since their political and moral culture was not yet equal to that of Christians. He was challenged in this view by his own special counsellor on Jewish affairs, von Eberstein: "It is always unjust to tie someone's hands and feet and then complain that he does not want to walk."

At the same time, Dalberg was under pressure from Paris to reorganize public life in Frankfurt in conformity with the *Code Napoleon* and the Declaration of the Rights of Man. It began to emerge that one reason for Dalberg's delay in implementing these rights was his desire to extract a price for them. Rothschild had suspected as much from the start. He intimated to Dalberg that the Jews of Frankfurt were prepared to pay for their rights; a long and complicated negotiation ensued.

It was characteristic of Frankfurt, where, as Schiller once put it, money reigned supreme, that the solution to the city's ancient problem of civic equality would, in the final resort, be a matter of haggling over payment. What was essentially a question of human rights, of recompense for centuries of injustice, became a question of money.

Rothschild may have hoped that the new Grand-Duke would be content with a personal gratuity; he soon discovered that he would not. Dalberg's administration owed a lot of money to the French government and was looking for funds to cover these debts. Dalberg's official excuse for demanding money was that he was entitled to "compensation" for the revenue he would lose if the medieval tax on Jews ("protection money") was abolished. The current income from that tax amounted to some 25,000 gulden annually.

Dalberg rejected all comparisons with France, where equal rights had been granted without charging money for them. If equal citizenship were granted, he claimed, the city would lose a considerable sum. During the next twenty years that loss might amount to nearly 1,000,000 gulden. In the spirit of the new liberal age, however, he was ready to forego compound interest and be content with a more modest sum: 500,000 gulden in cash.

Rothschild was in no position – or mood – to stand on principle. He bargained Dalberg down to 440,000 gulden, still a very high price. The Jews of Frankfurt were willing to raise it, especially as Rothschild offered to advance 100,000 gulden, almost a quarter of the total sum. Meanwhile, Rothschild held out for easier terms. Dalberg delayed his signature on the decree until there was agreement on them.

Rothschild's patience was running out. He wanted at least a public statement upholding the principle of civic equality. In January 1811, he wrote another obsequious and at the same time self-assured letter in pidgin German, to one of Dalberg's top aides. He had an office full of clerks fluent in four languages, who might have written this letter for him as they wrote many others. Instead, with something like nonchalance, he wrote in his own scarcely legible hand:

> I am constantly asked by the entire Jewish community how things stand. I should be very pleased if I could be the first messenger of the good news to our Nation, that His Royal Highness, our most gracious Lord and Grand-Duke, has put his signature [on the decree] . . . I confess I abuse your goodness and grace, but I do not doubt that heavenly rewards will await His Highness and his honored family, good fortune and blessings for, in truth, our whole Jewry will very gladly pay the charges [imposed on them] for the happiness to obtain equal rights.

Two weeks later, in the Official Gazette of 7 February 1811, Dalberg formally proclaimed the equality of all residents of Frankfurt under the law on condition, however, that no loss was caused thereby to the city's revenue. For this reason, Jews would be granted equal rights only after "the business of commutation" was successfully concluded. This would take almost another full year.

On 11 December 1811 Dalberg wrote to Rothschild:

> Worthiest Mr Court-Agent,
>
> You are a trustworthy upright man and you have spoken with all possible passion and a noble heart, for the good of your community. You have moved me so deeply that I have agreed to moderate my conditions as follows
>
> 1. For this year 1811 the general revenue office will be content with a cash payment of 150,000 fl.
>
> 2. Another 50,000 fl. in cash delayed until the end of 1813.
>
> 3. As of that date, the remaining 240,000 fl. in annual installments with 5% interest.

Two days later, Rothschild wrote to one of his sons that he had just returned back from Aschaffenburg, Dalberg's residence, where he

Karl Theodore von Dalberg (1744–1817), Grand Duke of Frankfurt, painted by an unknown artist. Rothschild continued to remind him of his past promises. Oil painting, 1810. (*Courtesy Jewish Museum, Frankfurt.*)

had devoted his time for an entire week to Jewish Community matters. He added proudly: "You are now a citizen!"

On 28 December, Dalberg finally signed the decree establishing equal rights. The news was received with joy in the Judengasse and with indignation in the rest of the city. A writer in *Sulamith*, the local Jewish family magazine, waxed:

Great is the joy of the Jews over the improvement of their unsatisfactory situation and [it is] easy to explain. Already many are registering to join the new National Guard. All are filled with ardent desire to prove their availability to the State.

Siegmund Geisenheimer, Rothschild's chief accountant, wrote to his father:

I am sending you today's Official Gazette in which we receive civic rights. Although it costs a lot of money, and perhaps another 30 Carolin on my share, I thank God for it.

In the Christian city, some of the old patrician merchants felt "as though the end of the world was near". With horror they expected a "black locust swarm" of Jews to displace them from all positions of primacy and control. Nor were liberals entirely happy. Wilhelm von Humboldt, who played an important part in the battle for Jewish emancipation, later confessed "I like Jews only *en masse*; *en detail* I strictly avoid them". It was at once suggested that Dalberg had been bought. German nationalists despised him anyway because of his collaboration with the French invader. An Austrian diplomatic agent reported that Dalberg had received a bribe of 33,000 Carolin (330,000 gulden). A French agent told the Duke of Rovigo, Napoleon's chief of police, that it had been through Rothschild that the Jews of Frankfurt achieved civic equality. "The Grand-Duke scarcely ever refuses him a request."

Throughout the months of struggle for civil rights, only Amschel was at home with his father. Calmann and Salomon, though the latter suffered from terrible backaches, were travelling back and forth between Frankfurt and Prague. Jacob was shuttling between Dunkirk, Paris and London. Buderus kept the Landgrave informed of Jacob's exertions on his behalf:

The young Rothschild is actually on his way to London to fetch the certificates of title regarding your capital investment ... On my advice Crown-Agent Rothschild has called in the capital payment due at Copenhagen and has received 159,600 gulden. Will your Electoral Highness graciously permit me to convey to him your Highness's satisfaction regarding his manifold activities on your behalf? I am informed by him that the Prague police have discovered the secret compartments in his carriage. I have therefore thought it advisable not to send my account for last month ... as it cannot be concealed under the clothes as letters can.

In 1809, Rothschild's three elder sons had jointly bought an empty plot of land, at the ruined northern end of the Judengasse, for 9,284 gulden. On this plot they built a fine new four-story stone house and Rothschild's offices and store rooms were moved in. It was only a few yards from the burnt-out ruin of the old *Hinterpfann*. From here Rothschild co-ordinated his far-flung sons. His astonishing concentration on business continued as before. Dispatch riders came and went all the time. Clerks, daughters-in-law and other attendants were on call. Most of the business by now was in banking. In the cellars there was a fairly large stock of wine which produced no income but was a common form of investment at the time. Rothschild had mellowed and was even emotional, especially towards his youngest son, Jacob, who had just joined Nathan in London. Rothschild wrote:

> You cannot imagine, my dear, the sensation your safe and good arrival has made upon us, for that the more as we believed your journey both dangerous and disagreeable,

Then, immediately, the old single-minded self:

> May your presence there be pleasant and as useful to you as to your parents, *by making good affairs and projecting [new] ones* ... I pray put your brother in mind that I desire him, always, to forward [to Frankfurt] every object which is able to give profit here.

A few months later, again to Jacob:

> P.S. Your dear mother sends her motherly love and asks me to tell her Jacob that according to his enquiry she expresses the following wishes 2 dozen ivory handle dessert knives and carving knife and fork also a coffee tray, everything in conformity with your good taste.

The Landgrave's investments called for constant attention. The vast sums Nathan was administering in London on his behalf were channeled through Frankfurt. The Landgrave's routine suspicions that everyone was cheating him were tedious and time consuming, but the time spent on them was well spent: "One gains the impression that the Landgrave's capital was the very foundation on which not only the Rothschilds' Frankfurt bank, but also their great international house, was built", Josef Sauer wrote in his *History of the Finances of the Landgraves of Hesse-Kassel*. To better protect Buderus from being harassed by the French police, Rothschild convinced Dalberg to give him a formal appointment in his administration. Amschel was Rothschild's right hand on these matters. Deferential and meticulous, Amschel was always glad to be of use. The old man was equally pleased with Salomon:

> Salomon is most pleasant company. Whenever I am worried, in a minute or so he seems to be able to enrich me by a million.

The new offices were comfortable, airy and well-lit. There was a large apartment on the top floor but Rothschild remained down the street in "The House at the Green Shield". Guttle continued to oversee the austere household. Their riches had in no way altered their modest way of life. The men's shirts were still worn until threadbare. Several times a day Rothschild walked up and down the half-ruined Judengasse. It was his one exercise. He used to say: "I go on writing, so as not to forget how to write, and walking in order to keep my legs moving."

In his personal life he remained rooted in the former ghetto. He could live anywhere he wanted – in a fine town house on the fashionable *Zeil* or, like Bethmann, in a Schloss outside the city gate – but he would not leave the old house in the Judengasse. For Guttle, moreover, leaving it would have been absolutely unthinkable. Their children were gradually assimilating into the surrounding gentile world. Amschel and Salomon were living in the Christian city with their families. Yet the old man never broke with orthodox Jewish custom. He admonished his sons:

A man has to think before he acts. But after having thought matters over everything else has to be left to God.

Taste and diet prevented him from sharing a meal with a Christian. Marie Belli-Gontard, married to the son of a well-known Frankfurt banker, remembered a luncheon party at her father-in-law's house:

> During the meal, the old Rothschild, who had business deals with my father-in-law, was announced. He was a fairly tall man, he wore a round, unpowdered wig and a small beard on the chin, the complete Jewish type. His eyes mirrored intellect and good will. He possessed both qualities. Greeting us warmly, he entered. The servant brought him a chair. He did not sit down. "Please sit down", said my father-in-law. "No, Sir", Rothschild responded, "I know what is becoming for me". "If you'll not sit down", said my father-in-law, "I'll also stand up". At this, Rothschild placed himself on the edge of the chair; we feared that he might fall off. This was the man who through industry founded a world power of finance.

He had been contemplating a new branch office in Paris for some time. There were political as well as commercial reasons for doing so. Paris was now the most important capital on the continent. Napoleon, after his marriage to Marie-Louise, the defeated Austrian Emperor's daughter, was at the zenith of his power. The parent firm in Frankfurt and Nathan's in London needed an absolutely reliable representative in Paris. Rothschild's youngest son, Jacob, seemed a good choice. He had long proved his abilities. At nineteen, he was sociable, open-minded and bold. Of the five sons, only he had been educated by an emancipated tutor. He probably spoke a little French and was as anxious as Nathan had been in his time to get out of Frankfurt to make his place in the big world.

An opportunity to supply him with the best letters of introduction had offered itself unexpectedly in March 1811. Dalberg wished to attend the baptism in Paris of the *Roi de Rome*, the new-born son of Marie-Louise and Napoleon. State visits were costly and Dalberg lacked the necessary cash. He applied to several Frankfurt merchants for a loan. For apparently political reasons, they refused his request. Rothschild immediately lent Dalberg 80,000 gulden and received in return a passport for Jacob and introductions to French treasury officials. Jacob soon after departed. He stopped briefly at Dunkirk on the English channel where he may have met Nathan for a short consultation. With their old father's blessing, the two brothers were preparing their biggest coup yet.

Nathan's illicit export of English goods to the continent had largely come to an end in 1810 as the result of new French policy. Napoleon's Edict of Trianon (5 August), relaxing the strict provisions of the continental blockade, had in effect legalized trade with England by imposing tariffs as high as 40–50 per cent, the equivalent of the smugglers' premium in the past. At the same time, the French decided to teach the merchants of Frankfurt a lesson they would never forget. The city was filled with English goods that had been smuggled in through Dutch, Scandinavian and Russian ports. In October, two French regiments occupied Frankfurt and sequestered these goods. Some were publicly burned. Heavy fines were imposed. No fewer than 234 Frankfurt firms were affected. Rothschild was number sixty-eight on this list (forty-one, according to another source). He was fined 19,348 francs, considerably less than others. Bethmann was fined 363,000 francs; Hebenstreit nearly 1,000,000. The incident elicited a rare letter of appreciation from the Landgrave. "I note with pleasure that the House of Rothschild has shown its traditional devotion to Me even in the present catastrophe at Frankfurt", he wrote Buderus. "You will kindly convey to them my satisfaction and gratitude."

From this date on, the House of Rothschild's trade in goods of all kinds sharply declined. Nathan was leading it to more lucrative fields; he was beginning to play an active role in the English war effort and Rothschild's decision to send Jacob to Paris was closely connected with this.

An English expeditionary force, under Wellington, was in Portugal fighting French troops, and in "terrible need of funds". Try as it might, the government in London was unable to meet these needs.

Soldiers' pay was in arrears and many had resorted to looting. This damaged Wellington's efforts to encourage the local population to rebel against French rule. He complained that some of his wounded officers in a hospital in Salamanca had been forced to sell their clothes simply to stay alive. He was borrowing money from shady Maltese and Italian bankers at outrageously usurious rates, in exchange for bills drawing on the British government in London.

Through agents in Malta, Marseilles and Livorno, Rothschild and his sons bought many of these bills at a fraction of their nominal value. Jacob transported them to London where Nathan cashed them at the Bank of England at huge profit. Early in 1811, Wellington grew desperate. He threatened to abandon his strategically crucial campaign at the rear of Napoleon's main army and withdraw from the peninsula.

At this point of great distress in London, Nathan Rothschild, having already amassed a small fortune through the sale of Wellington's bills of exchange, offered his services to the English government. He had just bought £800,000 worth of gold at a bargain price from the East India Company. (His credit must have been exceptionally good, or he might not have been able to raise this enormous sum.) Upon learning of Nathan's purchase, the government sent for him and said that they must have it for the Duke of Wellington. Nathan agreeably sold his gold to the government. "When they had it", Nathan later remembered, *"they did not know how to get it to Portugal. I undertook all that"*. He presented an audacious plan whereby the House of Rothschild, with its extensive network of family contacts, creditors and agents on the continent, would supply Wellington with the money he needed to continue his campaign. Rothschild & Sons would also be responsible for transporting the gold across enemy lines into the peninsula.

John Charles Herries, army Chief-Commissary, eagerly accepted Nathan's scheme. The Chancellor of the Exchequer approved it. Why, in the world's leading financial center, Herries had to wait for Nathan to save him is a mystery to this day. Why, if he needed it, had he not bought up the East India Company's gold himself? The reason why the world's greatest sea power was unable to supply its leading general with funds is a puzzle that cannot easily be resolved even now. It has been suggested that government in England at that time was in the hands of aristocratic martinets lacking all familiarity with the practical mechanics of daily life. Be this as it may, Nathan's blockade-runners immediately began to ship England's gold to his brothers on the French controlled coast. Nathan's courier system functioned with clockwork precision. Jacob or Salomon received the gold at Gravelines, Boulogne or Dunkirk and carried it to Paris. Jacob had quietly settled there early in March 1811.

Jacob's beginnings in Paris were more difficult than Nathan's had been in England. Unlike Nathan, who through his marriage, had been "adopted and supported by a rich and powerful clan", Jacob had to depend solely on his own wits and relatively limited resources. Nor was there a well-organized Jewish community in Paris. Jacob had only Dalberg's introductions, of which little if anything is known. We do know he quickly established a close rapport with leading French bankers. Among them were Guillome Mallet and Jean-Conrad Hottinguer, both Protestants of Swiss origin. By the shared bonds of a minority religion they were, like the Rothschilds, in possession of extensive but discreet credit facilities. In exchange for his English gold, they supplied Jacob with bills on Spanish and Portuguese banks. Wellington could cash these bills with little difficulty and at a helpful saving to the English Treasury.

Since very substantial transfers of gold coins were involved, it was inevitable that the French authorities would soon become aware of them. They were, however, shrewdly camouflaged as the capital transfers of continental capitalists, who had lost confidence in England's future and were fleeing the pound sterling, prepared even to take losses of 30 per cent in the process. The ruse may have been Jacob's idea. François Nicolas de Mollien, Napoleon's treasury minister, was completely taken in by it.

This is obvious from a letter Mollien sent Napoleon on 26 March. Mollien informed the Emperor of the massive influx of English gold and added:

> A Frankfurter, now living in Paris with a Frankfurt passport, named Rotschild [sic], is principally occupied with the transport of guineas from the English coast to Dunkirque; in a

single month he has brought in 100,000 guineas [£105,000]. In Paris he is in rapport with excellent bankers, such as Mallet, Charles Duvillier and Hottinguer. They supply him with bills of exchange on London. He maintains that according to letters, dated 20 March, which have just reached him from London, the intention there is to prevent the export of gold and silver coins by raising the price of the piaster from 5 to 5$^1/_2$ shillings and the price of guineas from 21 shillings to 30.

Such overvaluation of the English currency, Mollien claimed, was the equivalent of counterfeiting and would bring about its ruin. He added triumphantly: "*Fasse le ciel*, may heaven grant us, that Rotschild [sic] is well informed and that the blindness of ministers in London has gone that far."

Throughout the summer and fall of 1811, while the French treasury viewed the influx of guineas with pleasure as an indication of England's imminent decline, Jacob re-directed these same funds, as though with the cooperation of the French government, into the war-chest of Wellington, Napoleon's most tenacious foe. The other Rothschilds collected French specie in Germany, which were also transmitted by Jakob to Wellington. It has been claimed that between 1811 and 1815 almost £20,000,000 was transferred by the Rothschilds to Wellington, and to England's allies on the continent. Their profits from this business alone must have been immense

The French police never lost sight of Jacob and several of his letters to Nathan were intercepted. Orders went out to follow his every move. The police in Dunkirk requested his "eloignement" (removal); but this was not acted upon. A senior military official warned Napoleon that contrary to what Mollien thought, the English government might be behind Rothschild brothers' gold transports. The Emperor believed that his finance minister understood such things better than his generals. The French police persisted in its efforts to get to the bottom of the Rothschilds' many affairs. The chief of the French police in Mainz, Hubert, was asked to report on the elder Rothschild's "political disposition" and on his commercial rapport within and outside the empire. Hubert's report shows that there was little the French did not know, or guess, about Rothschild's intimate links with Dalberg and the exiled Landgrave. Since the sequestration of English goods in Frankfurt 1810, Hubert reported, the elder Rothschild's main business was banking. "As for his political attitudes, they are not the best. He certainly dislikes the French, even though he feigns loyalty to the French government."

Nathan's gold transports continued to arrive in Boulogne, Dunkirk or Gravelines on the channel coast, and in Amsterdam or Hamburg. The brothers took turns receiving them and transporting them on to their destinations. From 1812 these shipments also included England's subsidies for her continental allies. They were channeled to Berlin or Vienna through the parent firm in Frankfurt.

The itinerant brothers were spinning more than one scheme at a time and their old father was finding it increasingly difficult to keep up with all of them. He was often bed-ridden. Amschel stepped in to replace him whenever he could. The brothers coordinated their activities according to the scheme laid down for them by the old man. Copies of letters they wrote were circulated among the others. From his bed, Rothschild tried to supervize their affairs. Calmann spent the entire month of March 1812 between Paris and Gravelines and then returned to Frankfurt. Salomon replaced him in July and remained in Paris and on the channel coast until the end of September. A French police report described the two brothers as:

> extremely fine, extremely prudent, they know the art of making friends. One of their brothers is now in London. The Rothschild brothers in Paris maintain that they are authorized by the [French] government to entertain ... commercial relations with him.

Jacob had obviously won the esteem of Mollien and others in the Paris business world. He was flamboyant and warm-hearted and a little in love with Nathan's wife Hannah, to whom he wrote charming long letters in *Judendeutsch* addressed to "My dear sister". In the post-script of a business letter from Gravelines, where he was waiting for a consignment of Nathan's gold, he wrote:

I send a little dog for my good Anthony [Nathan's and Hannah's two year old son], let me know if he likes it.

In the fall of 1811, Rothschild fell seriously ill. By November he was well again. At this stage he could only be marginally involved in his sons' affairs. He also knew that French agents were carefully watching his every move. In an unsigned letter he sent to Jacob on 13 December 1811, he obliterated certain words which might have been compromising if the letter were to fall into the hands of the French police. (struck through words indicate where Rothschild obliterated the text):

> I send my love, dear Jacob. We received many times already ~~Paris bills~~ from Hamburg. In each case the despatch note did not arrive ... It seems that the ~~police~~ open the letters ... It may come, God forbid, to an interrogation. For this reason, dear son, I wish that you should find out from the merchants with whom you are friendly, whether it is permitted to send ~~Paris bills~~ ... and if I should be asked why I need this much ~~Paris bills, can I answer~~ that I send them in fact to the merchants?
>
> Is no risk involved in (admitting this)? ... Write to me with your opinion. Destroy the letters which you don't need. Langbein [codename for Nathan] thinks that he alone has to do all the thinking. Well, nobody gets anything for nothing.

Early in February 1812, Rothschild's name is on the list of the first nineteen heads of Jewish families who formally swore their oath of citizenship to the burgomaster of Frankfurt, Guiollette. They were finally equal citizens. Soon after, a couple of seats fell vacant on the Frankfurt electoral college, the body charged with choosing the city *prefect* which Dalberg filled with Rothschild and his old patrician rival, the banker Simon Moritz von Bethmann. Rothschild's appointment struck many people in Frankfurt as a shocking violation of sacred "German rights". But for the time being they could do nothing to prevent it.

The details of Rothschild's last months of life are fragmentary. His health continued to decline. Amschel was at his side at all times. In

Emancipation. The first page of the Frankfurt Civil Register for Jews (1812),
listing nineteen Jewish heads of families who swore their oath of allegiance
as equal citizens. Rothschild's is No. 17. It was characteristic of Frankfurt
where, as Schiller once put it, money reigned supreme, that in the final resort,
civic equality was granted only in exchange for payment. (*Courtesy Jewish
Museum, Frankfurt.*)

the *comptoir*, Amschel carried out his father's instructions. At home, Guttle, and their youngest daughter Jettchen, tended the painful wound that was causing him so much suffering and discomfort.

He remained active in the affairs of the Jewish community. As equal citizen, Jews were now conscripted to serve in Napoleon's army. This created social and other problems that Rothschild was called upon to resolve. The Frankfurt contingent of the Grande Armée went into action against the Russians between Bialystok and Vilnius, in the north-eastern corner of Poland. Early in March 1812, Amschel wrote to Nathan in London, informing him that their father was in Aschaffenburg for a meeting, presumably with Dalberg, "because things with the conscription are getting very difficult. Many have been conscripted. Father has therefore to do his part".

In August he briefly turned from his sons' huge transactions to his earliest love, rare silver and gold coins. To please Dalberg he offered him a collection of "303 extraordinarily beautiful" pieces for only 5,500 gulden, at no profit to himself.

Like everyone else in Frankfurt, he followed with great suspense the great drama of Napoleon's advance into the heart of the Russian empire. In August he was ill again. He did not live to see Napoleon's defeat. On 16 September 1812 – it was the Day of Atonement – Rothschild walked to the synagogue early in the morning. He spent the entire day there, mostly on his feet, praying and had been fasting since the previous evening. After dark, upon returning home to break the fast, he felt ill and was put to bed. On the following morning, he insisted on getting up and out to visit his son. As he walked down the Judengasse for the last time he felt great pain "in the region of his wound" and collapsed in the street. He was carried back to the house where his condition grew worse. He called in a lawyer and revised his will.

His main concern in his last hours was to secure the continued happiness and prosperity of his sons. He knew that riches came and went. He had seen in his lifetime fortunes dissipate through waste, vanity or infighting among heirs. Jewish fortunes, he warned Amschel:

do not keep longer than two generations. For two reasons: one, because house-keeping and other expenses are not considered; two, because of Jewish stupidity.

In his will he avoided the disclosure of his total assets by simply selling his shares in the business and all his other possessions to his five sons for a nominal sum of 190,000 gulden to be disbursed for the benefit of his wife Guttle and his five daughters. He reconfirmed his old rule that only the sons, in five equal shares, would inherit the family business. Oddly enough he left nothing to Jewish charity but "bequeathed the sum of one hundred gulden to three laudable mild Christian foundations". He urged his "dear children to relate to one another with mutual love and friendship". He knew his sons were strong-willed, difficult, impulsive men. He was afraid of their tempers. On his deathbed he urged them once more to remain united at all cost. It had become an obsession with him. According to Amschel, he said on his deathbed:

> Amschel, keep your brothers together and you will become
> the richest men in Germany.

The will concluded with a further warning against disunity. "Any undutiful child that disobeys this my fatherly will or disturbs my [other] sons in the calm exercise of their activity" would inherit only the legal minimum stipulated in the Napoleonic Code, computed on the basis of the 190,000 gulden. From this bare minimum, everything that child had received during his life would be further deducted.

He was dying, biblically, "full of days, riches and honor". Guttle and his daughters were at his side, but of his sons, only Amschel and (perhaps) Calmann. He begged them to be charitable and remain faithful to the religion of their forefathers and forbade all ostentation during his funeral. He knew it would pass through the Judengasse, the place which had been the defining, moulding fact of his life in a cold and hostile world and had furnished his imagery of it. In the twilight of consciousness he may have remembered his early days there. Now he was leaving it, but before his departure he had changed it radically. The new freedom he had helped to achieve emphasized the remoteness of the world into which he was born.

The end came suddenly. Two days after signing his revised will, in the early evening of 19 September 1812, he died. The funeral took place at noon on the following day. Women and children lined the Judengasse. Nearly all the men in the community walked behind the simple bier. His material success, his achievements for himself, his family and for the community as a whole, had endowed him with an aura of the hero. The bier was carried to where the grave had been dug in the ancient cemetery at the bottom of the Judengasse. In keeping with his wishes there were no speeches. It was a Sunday and the prayers of the mourners were drowned by the ringing of church-bells. He was buried next to his ancestor Isaak Elchanan (d. 1585), the first whose tombstone was marked with the emblem of a shield.

Rothschild's tombstone, as found after the Second World War in the ruins of the Jewish cemetary. (*Photograph by Klaus Meier-Ude, Frankfurt.*)

Most of the tombstones in the ancient cemetery were broken up by the Nazis in 1938. Photograph, *c.* 1949. (*Courtesy Jewish Museum, Frankfurt.*)

CHAPTER SEVEN

Aftermath

I N THE DAYS IMMEDIATELY following Rothschild's death it was his charity and human warmth that drew attention and grief. The official *Memorbuch* hailed his role as head of the relief for the poor, dearly loved by his brothers for his achievements. His greatest contribution to the community had been his attainment of "our freedoms in the present generation and in those to come".

The precariousness of these freedoms was reflected in their abrogation soon after the fall of Napoleon and in an obituary notice published soon after Rothschild's death, a small privately printed brochure entitled:

Exemplary Life

of

the late Banker Herr Mayer Amschel Rothschild
dedicated to all friends of virtue

Its author felt impelled to emphasize that Rothschild's life had proved "irrefutably that a Jew, as a Jew, is capable of being an excellent human being and a good citizen". The precepts of the Talmud were not "in contradiction to the laws of morality".

For those at his bedside little of this was important. Their loss was personal. His widow continued for many years to sign her letters "Guttle, wife of rabbi Mayer Amschel Rothschild". Of the brothers, Amschel was most affected by his father's death. He was now head of the bank in Frankfurt. The brothers prospered. According to records in the French National Archive, their combined capital grew from 3,332,000 francs in 1815 to 118,458,332 in 1828. By 1830 they were not only among the richest in Germany, as Rothschild had foreseen, but in all of Europe – the inventors of multi-national *haute finance*, the new force which gave impetus to capitalism throughout the nineteenth century. They reached this point by their own efforts, but their father had shown them the way. In their letters to each other the brothers continued to evoke Rothschild's memory.

Amschel was especially dedicated to this task. Every year, on the eve of the anniversary of their father's death, he wrote to his brothers and nephews to remind them of the excellent qualities of the founder of their House: "My dear brothers, our father of blessed memory, used to say . . ."

When, in 1817, the Rothschild brothers were made noblemen by the Austrian Emperor, the coveted appellation *von* was issued not to them but (five years after his death) to "Mayer Amschel von Rothschild and his descendents of both sexes". This may have been an oversight, but it must have given the brothers, and especially Amschel, immense pleasure. Within a few years they would be made barons. Each owned shares in the others' businesses. But the five branches – A. M. Rothschild & Sons (Frankfurt), N. M. Rothschild (London), Rothschild Freres (Paris), S. M. Rothschild (Vienna), C. M. Rothschild (Naples) – remained linked. Their balance sheets were consolidated each year into a single account.

The brothers spoke German, English, French and Italian, though always with strong accents. Amschel, Jacob and Calmann gentrified their names to Anselm, James and Carl. In the heyday of nationalism they constituted a truly European family. This was rare in nineteenth-century Europe. Bismarck, Talleyrand, Metternich and Napoleon the Third visited them in their fairy-tale palaces. Unlike other assimilated Jews they emphasized, even flaunted, their ethnicity and religion. By their social success they proved that for Jews money was a better entrance-ticket to society than baptism, as Heine wrongly assumed. (Heine may have had the Rothschilds in mind when he made his celebrated remark that he would never have converted to Christianity if the law allowed one to steal silver spoons.)

Their late father had exhorted them on his deathbed to remain united, which they did for decades, though they often quarrelled and hurled insults at each other – "ass", "stupid", "you make me sick" or "you are acting like a drunkard". Major transactions were the subject of joint discussions. The quiet, meticulous Amschel, the

The five Rothschild brothers, based on a painting by Moritz Daniel
Oppenheim. Lithograph, 1852. (*Courtesy Historical Museum, Frankfurt.*)

guardian of tradition, kept reminding them of their father's injunction to remain "united, [with] a common till, we have to work together without quarrels".

Amschel succeeded his father as head of the parent company. He enjoyed his fine new house and garden outside the former ghetto, as only a man who had grown up inside would: it was "a paradise", with flowers and fresh air and room for a big family; yet to his deep chagrin, he remained childless. Amschel gave "big diplomatic dinners but ate [kosher food] before, prepared by his own cook". In the eyes of Michelet his face was as striking as "a sketch by Rembrandt, with the profile of an intelligent monkey". Bismarck mocked his accent but enjoyed his company. Nathan's son Anthony complained that uncle Amschel was such "a regular bother asking me about getting married and writing to uncle Salomon that I only waited till his death to marry a Christian".

Nathan remained in London, "perhaps the greatest figure ever to adorn the international capital markets, greater even than J. P. Morgan and Michael Milken in their primes". Marked by the grace and independence of mind produced by wealth and a long sojourn in England, Nathan, unlike his brothers, displayed little if any interest in titles.

Curiosity about him and the other Rothschilds was obsessive. It was fashionable to believe that bankers were the ultimate oligarchy, the decisive repository of power. As early as 1818, Byron wrote:

> *Who hold the balance of the world? Who reign*
> *O'er congress whether royalist or liberal?*
> *Who rose the shirtless patriots of Spain?*
> *Who keep the world, both old and new, in pain*
> *Or pleasure? Who make politics run glibber all?*
> *The shade of Buonaparte's double daring?*
> *Jew Rothschild and his fellow-Christian Baring!*

Nathan was the most active, the most successful of the brothers and the most domineering. His brothers deferred to him. Salomon wrote "You are the general and we are your lieutenants". He had a robust sense of humor. Prince Pückler-Muskau came to see him on urgent business. Nathan was busy. He offered him a chair and asked him to wait. The Prince said, "I do not think you heard who I am. I am the Prince Pückler-Muskau". Nathan looked up from his work and said: "Well, take two chairs."

He was single-minded in his pursuit of business and more business. At a dinner in 1834 someone with the snobbish frame of mind produced by inherited wealth expressed a hope that his children were not too attached to business. On the contrary, Nathan answered:

> I wish them to give mind and soul, and heart, and body, and
> everything to business; that is the way to be happy. It requires
> a great deal of boldness and a great deal of caution, to make
> a great fortune; and when you have got it it requires ten
> times as much wit to keep it.

Salomon settled in Vienna where, although an Austrian baron, as a Jew he could not own a house. He lived for years in a hotel close to the imperial palace, at first in a suite of rooms and eventually in the entire building.

Carl (Calmann) settled in Naples as court-banker of the Bourbon kingdom. James prospered in Paris. In 1820, he married his niece Betty, Salomon's daughter, the first of many endogamous marriages between members of the Rothschild family in the nineteenth century. Nearly two-thirds of Mayer Amschel Rothschild's grand children married each other. The object of these carefully planned and solemnly celebrated liaisons was not so much to keep the dowry within the family but, in compliance with their late grandfather's dynastic scheme, to strengthen the family's power and autonomy.

Perhaps because James lived in Paris, "the capital of the nineteenth century", or because of his lively personality, he inspired fantastic superlatives by writers from Heine to Balzac, Toussenel and Emile Zola – art, gossip and slander, fulsome paeans of praise and scurrilous pamphlets born of racism and sheer hatred, staples of nineteenth century antisemitic propaganda. In Heine's eyes he was no less than the "prophet" of a new religion, the religion of money. "How wondrous that once again it is the Jews who invent this new religion". Heine often visited James in his office where "the people, and not only the Chosen People but all the other Peoples of the world, bow and pay obeisance to him".

> This Nero of finance who built himself a golden palace on the rue Lafitte from where he controls the stock exchanges as an absolute ruler, is like his predecessor, the Roman Nero a violent destroyer of aristocratic privilege and (with Richelieu and Robespierre) one of the greatest revolutionaries who laid the foundations of modern democracy.

From this feuilletonistic hyperbole – if not downright nonsense – by a poet who meant to pay Rothschild a compliment, it was not a big step, later on, to the lethal insinuations of a worldwide conspiracy.

Rothschild's widow Guttle survived him by thirty-seven years. She refused to move out of the old house in the Judengasse where as the wife of a modest moneychanger she had raised her numerous sons and daughters. She was certain that if she left the "House at the Green Shield" she would bring bad luck upon her sons. "Here in this house I have seen them become rich and powerful", she said. "It would be presumptuous, if in my old age I would leave my humble hut."

In Rothschild's lifetime she had been a loving figure in the background. After his death she became a celebrity. She was compared to Laetitia, Napoleon's mother, for giving birth to so many "financial Bonapartes". Guttle, or as she was now known, Gudule, sent her sons circular letters and they showered her with precious gifts. She continued to supply them with homemade shirts and cakes.

> Dear Jacob, concerning your shirts, I sent 5 and 10 sack-cloth shirts with the courier. I would have loved to deliver to you the others too . . . but the girl who is at work on them got engaged and this hindered her from making them.

> Dear Salomon, you cannot imagine with how much admiration your earrings and brooch were met. I wore them for the Bar Mitzvah dinner.

The fairy-tale element in Guttle's story appealed to Hans Christian Anderson who, after a visit to Frankfurt, wrote a moving little piece about her. Her sons visited her often. They had to walk part of the way through the mud of the Judengasse since their fine carriages were unable to reach the house. She received them upstairs in the window seat of her dark old parlor, wearing a lace cap and fanning herself with an ebony fan. They implored her to move to a larger home in a healthier part of town. She always refused. Leaving the

Guttle's window seat in the second floor parlor of the old house in the Judengasse. She resisted all attempts to induce her to vacate the house until her death in 1849. Photograph, 1925. (*Courtesy Hulton Deutsch Collection, London.*)

183

old house seemed to her a "sin". Her sons enlarged and refurbished the house as best they could and her grandchildren came and stayed with her. The street further deteriorated over the years. Jews hardly lived there anymore and, by 1835, it was lined mostly with the shops of rag dealers and other second-hand goods. From above came a dim light. Brides and bridegrooms who married into the Rothschild family were required to present themselves to Guttle. These were solemn occasions and reflected the family's unique perception of itself. At least two of the many weddings between Rothschild cousins actually took place in Guttle's house. Nathan died there in 1836 while attending the wedding of his eldest son Lionel Nathan to his niece Charlotte, Carl's daughter. Guttle survived her husband by thirty-seven years and her son Nathan by a decade. By mid-century, the Rothschild's "ancestral home" in the Judengasse had become a Frankfurt tourist attraction, together with Goethe's birth place in the Grosser Hirschgraben. At ninety-four, still lucid, Guttle spoke of acquiring a second house in the country. A Frankfurt woman is said to have come to her, saying "How terrible! War is breaking out". Guttle reassured her: "Don't be afraid. There will be no war. My sons will not provide the money for it." She became very frail – "I have had too many children", she told Marie Belli-Gontard, "the deepest well can run out of water" – but retained a good sense of humor. Her doctor assured her that she was in perfect health but she said: "Why should God have me at 96 when he can have me now at 94?" She died aged ninety-six in 1849.

Notes
Bibliography
Index

NOTES

The Rothschild Archive in London is identified in these notes as RAL.

A Note on Purchasing Power

"Consumer prices have risen by approximately 4,500 per cent between 1790 and the time of writing. Thus £1 in 1790 is roughly equivalent to £45 today (1996)" (p. 17): *Economist*, 22 February 1992, p. 88.

1. A Small Town in Germany

". . . if a great war was still possible in Europe if the House of Rothschild set their face against it" (p. 19). See J. A. Hobson, *Imperialism: A Study* (London, 1902), p. 64.

". . . he refused to call his age 'enlightened' and instead referred to it as 'barbaric'" (p. 21). See H. Graetz, *Geschichte der Juden* (Frankfurt, n.d.), XI, 45 ff.

". . . witnessed in his youth" (p. 23). See J. W. Goethe, *Wahrheit und Dichtung*, in Goethe's *Werke* (Stuttgart v. Leipzig, n.d.), vol. v, p. 85.

". . . We may make, do and deal with you as it pleases Us" (p. 25). Quoted in Horst Karasek, *Der Fedtmilch Aufstand. Wie die Frankfurter 1612/14 ihrem Rat einheitzten* (Frankfurt, 1969), p. 26.

". . . the equivalent of US$400,000)" (p. 25). See S. Krieg, *Frankfurter Burgerzwiste und Zustande im Mittelalter* (Frankfurt, 1864), p. 419.

". . . regulated the personal and professional lives of Frankfurt Jews down to minute details" (p. 26). See Friedrich Bothe, *Frankfurths wirtschaftliche-soziale Entwicklung* (Frankfurt, 1920), p. 261.

"Fines for violating these rules ranged from five to twenty thaler" (p. 27). See J. J. Schudt, *Neue Franckfurter Jüdische Kleiderordnung* (Franckfurt am Main, 1716), pp. 13–17.

". . . English goods at 25 per cent under the factory price" (p. 29). See H. Heine, *Gesammelle Werke* (Berlin, n.d.), vol. viii, p. 64.

"Malice and stupidity/Like street dogs used to mate./Their brood can still be recognized/By their sectarian hate" (p. 29). *Ibid, Deutschland ein Wintermarchen*, vol. iv.

". . . Mozart and his little sister Nannerl gave a concert at which the Goethes were present . . ." (p. 30). See Goethe, *Im Gespräch* 3.2.1830 (Zurich, 1944), p. 667.

". . . Jewish ladies and Christian gentlemen fell upon each other" (p. 32). Attributed to Goethe's friend Husgen, quoted in H. Voelker, *Die Stadt Goethe's, Frankfurt im 18. Jahrhundert* (Frankfurt, 1932), p. 275.

". . . completely ran out of this commodity" (p. 32). H. Heine über Ludwig Boerne; see Heine's *Gesammelle Werke*, vol. vii, p. 165.

". . . put there and maintained, as Goethe noted" (p. 33). See Goethe, *Wahrheit und Dichtung*, in *Werke*, vol. v, p. 84.

". . . 'In reason!', Mendelssohn answered" (p. 34). *Sulamith* (Jewish family magazine), Frankfurt 1812–5.

"The air was saturated with their calls" (p. 34). See N. Boyle, *Goethe, The Poet and the Age* (Oxford and New York, 1992), p. 48; Voelker, *op. cit.*, p. 71.

"... a frenzy of making money and spending it" (p. 35). Goethe to Schiller, 9 August 1797.

"I'd choose a typical metropolis . . . And on, past any gates resistance/The suburbs sprawl into the distance" (p. 35). See Goethe, *Faust II*, Act iv, translated by Walter Arndt (New York, 1976).

"Moreover, their girls were pretty . . ." (p. 36). See Goethe, *Dichtung v. Warhrheit*, i, iv.

"... somber, humid and filthy" (p. 39). See Bernard Müller, *Beschreibung des gegenwartigen Zustandes der Freien Reichsstadt Frankfurt* (Leipzig, 1795), p. 21.

"... one could easily smell it from a distance" (p. 40). Anon, *Reise durch Thüringen etc* (Leipzig, 1796).

"... the non-circumcised population there" (p. 40). Heine, *Samtl. Werke*, vii, 117.

"Sholet is the dish of heaven/Whose immortal recipe/God himself once gave to Moses/Long ago upon Mount Sinai" (p. 40). See *The Poetry and Prose of Heine*, translated by A. Kramer (New York, 1959), p. 266.

"... their names and the general modesty of their circumstances" (p. 43). See Alexander Dietz, *Stammbuch der Frankfurter Juden 1349–1849* (Frankfurt, 1907), p. 244ff.

"... the Jewish community of Frankfurt . . ." (p. 43). Jewish National and University Library, Jerusalem.

"He paid an annual tax of only eight gulden" (p. 43). Frankfurt City Archive, *Judenschätzungenregister 1725–1793*, fol. 178, 5 (now lost) but cited in Dietz, *Stammbuch der Frankfurter Juden* (Frankfurt, 1907), p. 244.

"His declared assets in 1749, a total of 1375 gulden . . ." (p. 47). See Christian Wilhelm Berghoeffer, *Meyer Amschel Rothschild* (Frankfurt, 1922), p. 172.

"... the other family was named Bauer . . ." (p. 48). See Dietz, *Stammbuch*, p. 464.

"... teachers per pupil in the ghetto than in the rest of the city" (p. 51). See H. Voelker (ed), *Die Stadt Goethes, Frankfurt am Main im XVIII. Jahrhundert* (Berlin, 1920), p. 104.

"... absolutism, mercantilism and baroque culture . . ." (p. 56). See Selma Stern, *The Court Jew* (Philadelphia, 1950), p. 11.

"... I hope you'll do your best" (p. 57). Quoted in H. Schnee, *Die Hoffinanz und der moderne Staat*, vol. iii, (Berlin, 1960), p. 102.

2. First Steps

"... suffer a fine" (p. 61). City edict of 24 February 1756, cited in Isidor Kracauer, *Geschichte der Juden in Frankfurt a.M. (1150–1824)* (Frankfurt, 1925–1927), pp. 416–7.

"... gifts of cash and jewellery to the imperial couple and their entourage" (p. 61). During the coronation of Francis II in 1790, the value of these forced gifts amounted to 11,019 gulden according to a list (nr 152) preserved in the files of the Jewish community archive (now lost) and quoted in Kracauer, *op. cit.*, p. 313. Specifically, the Jews of Frankfurt gave:

Silver gifts		3196
plus their wrappings and boxes		186
Cash (in gold ducats) for the Emperor	300	
the Empress	200	
the Archduke Franz	200	
the Imperial Courtier Albini	50	
the Imperial Courtier Pappenheim	30	
the Duke Rosenberg	12	
the Imperial Commissars	30	
total	832	4653

the agent Moses Coblenz	360
various gifts to other aides	800
tips to imperial servants	360
poem in honor of the Emperor	190
for confirmation of privileges	840
grand total 11019 gulden.	

"In Mainz and Mannheim and in [nearby] Hanau the parks are open [to Jews] . . . only we are denied [this right]" (p. 63). See Leon Poliakov, *History of Antisemitism*, III, p. 476.

"38 gulden 30 kreuzer to Jew Meyer for medals" (p. 64). State Archive, Marburg, *Rechnungen* II, Kassel (Chatoulkasse, 1764) No. 96.

". . . help me make my fortune here in the city of Frankfurt" (p. 65). *Ibid*, Personalien, Rothschild MStS 1711. Also in Berghoeffer, *Meyer Amschel Rothschild* (Frankfurt, 1922), pp. 8–9.

". . . bestow the title of Court-Factor upon the Protected Jew Meyer Amschel Rothschild of Frankfurt" (p. 65). Rothschild files in the Ozoby arkhiv, Moscow 637/1/4.

". . . perhaps six or seven more who died at birth or soon after" (p. 66). Stillbirths were not recorded at the time, nor were the deaths of very young children. Mortality in the over-crowded ghetto between 1735 and 1785 was 58 per cent higher than in the rest of Frankfurt. Over 50 per cent of the dead in the ghetto were children under the age of fifteen. The local doctor, S. A. Behrends, reported frequent epidemics of lung and skin diseases, dropsy fever and a mysterious "paralysis of the body". See Isidor Kracauer, *Geschichte der Judengasse in Frankfurt a.M.* (Frankfurt, 1922), p. 463ff; S. A. Behrends, *Der Einwohner in Frankfurt a.M. in Absicht auf seine Fruchtbarkeit, Mortalitat und Gesundheit geschildert* (Frankfurt, 1771), p. 235.

". . . antiques, medals and objects of display (p. 68). See S. J. Schroeck, *Handlungsschema von Frankfurt a.M.* (Frankfurt, 1778), p. 37.

"Meyer Amschel Rothschild/facteur de la Cour/Le prince hereditaire Landgrave de Hesse/Francfurt sur le Mayn (p. 70). Full text of this letter, now presumably lost, in *Frankfurter Zeitung* (3 December 1903) is a good example of Rothschild's odd use of language:

Gnädigster Herr Rath, die Vorige Woche Habe die Genad Gehabt von den Herrn Graffen sein Sekretär mich wiesend gemacht dass Euer Hochwohlgeboren, ein schönes Münzenkabinet besitzen und zur Kompledierung Täglich Mehres Ein kaufen. Dieses erkünet mich so frey zu sein Einliegende Catalogus Von Meine zu Verkauf habende Müntzen Einzusenden. Sollte Ew. Hochwohlgeb. ein Anzahl angenehme stücke um beistehende Preise erwählen und befehlen wirde sogleich unterthänigst einsenden. Auch bin ich willen Rechtens ein Catalogus Von denen jetzt Neue Erkaufte Müntzen von dem Hn. Gfn. auch ein Verzeichnis davon zu verfertigen solch sein zwahr Meinstens sächsische Müntzen und Medalien. Nach Erhalte Erlaubnis wirde den Catalogus einsenden. in Tiefster unterthänigkeit Behare mit höchster Consideration und Respekt Euer Hoch Wohlgeborne Mein gnädigster Rath unterthänigster Diener Meyer Amschel Rothschild mein adresse Meyer Amschel Rothschild, facteur de la Cour, Le prince hereditaire Landgrave de Hesse a Francfurt le Mayn.

Franckfurt 22 August 1780.

". . . income between 1771 and 1779 was 30,680 gulden, an annual average of

3,835 gulden (p. 71). Cited by Bertrand Gille, *Histoire de la maison Rothschild* (Geneva, 1965), p. 39.

". . . amounted to 2,400 gulden (p. 71). Cited by Nicholas Boyle, *Goethe: The Poet and the Age* (Oxford and New York, 1992), pp. 50–1.

". . . [the price of each being calculated] inclusive of recruiting and [burying the] corpse (p. 74). See Friedrich Kapp, *Der Soldatenhandel deutscher Fursten nach Amerika 1775–1783* (Berlin, 1864), p. 22, 41.

". . . profits in 1776 from such business were estimated at several millions (p. 74). See Josef Sauer, *Die Finanzgeschafte der Landesgrafen von Hessen-Kassel* (Fulda, 1930), p. 49.

". . . the reason for this was that I had been granted credit (p. 75). See Berghoeffer, *op. cit.*, p. 24.

". . . in a free Imperial and Commerce city like Frankfurt? (p. 76). See Cornelia Ruhlig and Jurgen Steen, *Stadt und Natur, Frankfurt im 1780* (Frankfurt, 1982), p. 157.

"Copies of the play's text were confiscated as blasphemous in a local book shop (p. 76). See Heuberger and Helga Krohn, *Hinaus aus dem Ghetto . . .* (Frankfurt, 1988), p. 16.

". . . it aroused neither terror nor pity (p. 76). See F. Hegel, *Early Theological Writings*, translated by T. M. Knox (New York, 1961), pp. 193–4, 204–5, 265.

". . . scoffing at the words of our sages (p. 77). Attributed to Pinhas Horowitz (Chief Rabbi 1771–1805); see Kracauer, *Geschichte der Juden in Frankfurt*, vol. II, p. 324, 327, 336.

". . . Rothschild was urgently needed in Hanau on Sundays (p. 77). See Sauer, p. 77; Alexander Dietz, *Frankfurter Handelsgeschichte*, iv/2 (Frankfurt, 1910), p. 725.

". . . politely but firmly refused (p. 77); "glimpflich abzulehnen sei", texts of Goethe's letter and senate resolution in G. L. Kriegk, *Deutsche Kulturbilder aus dem 18. Jahrhundert* (Leipzig, 1874), pp. 100–101.

". . . the teacher was ordered back into the Judengasse (p. 78). Frankfurt City Archive, Ugw. D33, No. 65; council resolution of 27 July 1790.

". . . the conclusion of mass in the Christian churches? (p. 78). Petition to senate, 21 June 1784, Frankfurt City Archive, Bestand Juden, Ugb D33.

"His assets at this time have been estimated at 150,000 gulden (p. 78). See Gille, *op. cit.*, p. 39.

"one of the best in the Judengasse (p. 78). See Dietz, *op. cit.*, p. 470.

". . . each particle of space was carefully turned to account (p. 80). See Count Egon Caesar Corti, *The Rise of the House of Rothschild*, translated by Brian and Beatrix Lunn (New York, 1928), p. 18.

". . . march him off to the main guard house as a common thief (p. 83). Frankfurt City Archive, Ugb D33 Nr.53.

". . . scarcely daring to beg their judges for mercy (p. 83). See N. Karamazin, *Letters of a Russian Traveller, 1780–1790*, translated by F. Jonas (New York, 1957), pp. 100–101. On Frankfurt fairs, see C. D. Ebeling and P. H. C. Brodhagen (eds), *Gottfried Christian Bohus wohlerfahrener Kaufmann* (Hamburg, 1789).

"They never demanded the removal of their chains; they were satisfied if the chains did not cut too deep (p. 83). See Kracauer, p. 426.

3. Patronage and Power

". . . estimated at between 40 and 120,000,000 gulden (p. 84). See Corti, p. 14.

". . . an exceptionally low price (p. 85). Berghoeffer, p. 23.

". . . by this time his English income alone amounted to £250,000 a year (p. 85). See Kapp, p. 49.

"According to one version, there were

seventy (p. 86). cf P. Losch, *Kurfurst Wilhelm I, Landgraf von Hessen* (Marburg, 1923), appendix xi; N. Vehse, *Geschichte der deutschen Höfe* (Leipzig, 1911), p. 266.

". . . Buderus's private investments produced handsome profits (p. 86). See Buderus's biography by his great grandson, *Lothar Buderus von Carlshausen, The life of a Hessian Public Official in Difficult Times* (in Hessenland, Monatsschrift für Landes-und Volkskunde Hessens, vol. 42, No. 2–3, February-March 1931).

". . . pay the highest price offered by anyone in Kassel (p. 87). See Berghoeffer, p. 24

"The Landgrave . . . authorized only £2,000 (p. 88). Ozoby arkhiv, Moscow 637/1/249.

". . . the hostility shown to his troops by the Jews of Frankfurt (p. 90). See Kracauer, *Frankfurt und die franzosische Republik 1795–1797*, in *Archiv fur Frankfurts Geschichte und Kunst*, III Folge, vol. 3, p. 156.

"Rothschild and his rivals were kept fully occupied in discounting the bills received from England in connection with this subsidy" (p. 90). See Corti, p. 14.

". . . fatherly good-will (p. 92). See Berghoeffer, p. 29.

". . . but could produce proof for only a few thousand (p. 92). See Dietz, *Frankfurter Handelsgeschichte*, vol. iv/2, p. 729.

". . . half as many again seem to have been lost (p. 93). Frankfurt City Archive, Criminal file no. 11025.

"By now he was 'more dead than alive', according to the protocol (p. 97). *Ibid*, interrogation of 30 August 1778, art. inq. 87.

". . . he suffered another deep personal humiliation, or 'molestation' (p. 97). See Salomon Jacob Cohen, *Musterhaftes Leben des verewigten Herrn Bankiers, Meyer Amschel Rothschild* (Frankfurt a.M., 1813), p. 16.

". . . the cash in my pocket never completely ran out (p. 98). H. Heine über Ludwig Boerne, *Samtliche Werke*, vol. 7 (Berlin, 1887), p. 256.

". . . all who seemed poor and hurried on in the dark (p. 98). The Frankfurt historian G. L. Kriegk, quoted in R. Ehrenberg, *Grosse Vermögen, Die Fugger, Rothschild* (Krupp. Jena, 1925), p. 57; see also Salomon Jacob Cohen, *op. cit.*, p. 17.

". . . live in a decent house in the Christian town (p. 99). The difficulty of attaining this privilege was exemplified at this time by the case of Dr Heymann Joseph Goldschmidt, a medical doctor who had made several applications to the senate asking for permission to live outside the ghetto. In the Judengasse, he claimed, there was no proper school for his children, nor could he hold a seminar there "on Kantian philosophy" which "friends of literature" in the city had asked him to give. "The sweet hope" of being granted his "humblest application" was not fulfilled. The senate decided to "reject the request once and for all". (Resolution of 11 June 1795, cited in Kracauer, *Judengasse*, p. 415.)

"When the fire started nobody could get into the [burning] locked houses and there were no Jews there to put out the fires (p. 99). Goethe's mother to her son in Weimar, 1 August 1796.

". . . declared a fortune of 420,000 gulden (p. 100). See Dietz, *Stammbuch*, p. 417.

"The lowest has been 60,000 gulden (p. 101). See Dietz, *Frankfurter Handelsgeschichte*, iv/2, p. 729.

". . . the highest 490,000 thousand (p. 101). See Gille, p. 39.

". . . confirms the higher estimate (p. 101). Rothschild file of 8 November 1797 in the Ozoby arkhiv, Moscow, 637/1/6.

". . . negotiating one of the Landgrave's loans to the city of Frankfurt (p. 102). See Sauer, p. 88.

"I will go to England. I could speak

nothing but German. On the Thursday I started (p. 103). See C. Buxton (ed), *Memoirs of Sir Thomas Fowell Buxton, Bt.* (London, 1848), p. 289.

4. A European Family

"Ruppel & Harnier hated Rothschild and the latter feared them (p. 105). See Berghoeffer, *op. cit.*, p. 85.

"Its [cruel] details were material for a drama (p. 105). See Dietz, *Frankfurter Handelsgeschichte*, iv/2, p. 675.

". . . exempt from all levies, poll-taxes and other surcharges imposed on [their] co-religionists (p. 107). Ozoby arkhiv, Moscow 637/1/249.

"The *kethuba* (p. 108). *Ibid*, 637/1/347.

"Rothschild had paid him one hundred louis d'ors for the honor (p. 108). RAL; Carl to Amschel, 1817.

". . . the wealth of the House of Rothschild already amounted to several million pounds sterling (p. 109). See H. Schnee, *Rothschild, Geschichte einer Finanzdynastie*, (Gottingen, 1961), p. 37.

"They call no man Infidel unless he be bankrupt (p. 109). Voltaire, *Letters Concerning the English Nation*, vi.

". . . his [kosher] dinner being cooked by a Jewess [was] taken to his warehouse every day (p. 110). See B. Williams, *The Making of Manchester Jewry 1740–1875* (Manchester, 1985), p. 19.

"You have brains but you did not learn to keep order . . . (p. 111). RAL T 2723.

". . . he only just became bar-mitzvah (p. 111). RAL T 271.

". . . a big warehouse [in Manchester] and a bridge over the Seine [in Paris] (p. 112). RAL T 241.

"Guttle, wife of the honoured Meyer Rothschild (p. 112). RAL T 273.

"Guttle, wife of Meyer Rothschild (p. 112). RAL T 272.

". . . they undertook nothing contrary to their prince's interests (p. 113). Leon Poliakov, *Les Banquiers Juives et la Saint*

Siege du XIII au XVII siecle (Paris, 1965), p. 148.

"Men of higher birth and rank, whom I do not have to name, used the same means [to get rich] and still use them to this day (p. 114). Lothar Buderus von Carlshausen, *op. cit.*, p. 38.

"It is possible that even greater sums and better conditions can be obtained from him (p. 117). See Ehrenberg, *op. cit.*, p. 34, 50.

". . . more than eight months earlier (p. 117). See Sauer, *op. cit.*, p. 93.

"Their comptoir is their church (p. 117). H. Heine, (Hrsg. Hugo Bieber) *Confessio Judaica, Eine Auswahl* (Berlin, 1925), p. 9.

". . . the prime position not only in Frankfurt but throughout Germany (p. 117). See Berghoeffer, p. 43.

". . . a significant sum of money (p. 118). *Ibid*, p. 40.

"Envy may speak against him, but he is a good man who deserves respect (p. 118). *Ibid*, p. 43.

". . . nowhere are so many people tortured by hemorrhoids as in the Judengasse (p. 118). Quoted in Kracauer, *Geschichte der Judengasse*, p. 413.

"The sitting position is detrimental to his health (p. 119). Frankfurt City Archive, Juden, Ugb D33 No. 99.

". . . donated 400 reichsthaler toward the construction of the new 'Neustadter church' (p. 119). Marburg State Archive, Nr. 19 Best. 16 xiv.

"Serene Prince Elector . . ." (p. 120). *Ibid*.

". . . more like stables, more like thieves' dens than human habitations (p. 121). Quoted in Geiger's *Zeitschrift zur Geschichte des Judentums*, 4/5, 1890–1892, p. 205.

". . . our city would not be as flourishing and important as it is now (p. 121). Quoted in *In Commemoration of the Frankfurt Jewish Community* (Jerusalem, 1965), p. 25.

"... half a day is saved (p. 121). Related by Miriam Rothschild, *Die Rothschilds, Beiträge zur Geschichte einer europäischen Familie* (Frankfurt, 1994), p. 151, 159.

"... Amschel assured the magistrate that no signs were hung nor were goods ever displayed outside (p. 121). Frankfurt City Archive, Act of 13 October 1803.

"*C'est une satisfaction que je demande pour la nation française!* (p. 122). Frankfurt City Archive, Uglb. D.33, No.97 and 120.

"... since they would be deprived of their daily bread (p. 122). See F. Bothe, *Geschichte der Stadt Frankfurt* (Frankfurt, 1913), p. 467.

"... a greater number of Jews to move from the Judengasse to healthier homes outside (p. 122). Archiv für Geschichte und Kunst in Frankfurt, 3. Folge, VI, p. 288.

"... Michael Hess, was head teacher (p. 124). *Festschrift zur Jahrhundertfeier der Realschule (Philantropin) zu Frankfurt a.M.*, 1904, pp. 6ff.

"It seems as though the Christian gentlemen begrudge Jews the light of knowledge and are downright eager to keep them in their ignorance (p. 124). Quoted in *Jüdisches Leben in Frankfurt* (Frankfurt, 1796–1818), vol. ii, p. 14.

5. Forging the Dynasty

"... irreconcilable with the security of France (p. 125). Cited in *Correspondence de Napoleon I*, vol. xiii (Paris, 1863), p. 588.

"With Buderus I was able to put many things aside (p. 125). Quoted in L. Buderus von Carlshausen, *op. cit.*, Heft 3, March 1931, p. 65.

"... cash vouchers and mortgage documents could then be smuggled out of the country (p. 127). Berghoeffer, *op. cit.*, p. 100.

"... the prince [after the war] made me a present of all his wine and his linen (p. 129). See Buxton (ed), *Memoirs of Sir Thomas Fowell Buxton* (London, 1848), p. 345.

"... adopts the name of von Carlshausen (p. 130). L. Buderus von Carlshausen, *op. cit.*, p. 65.

"He did not 'want to be a burden', he wrote (p. 130). Berghoeffer, *op. cit.*, p. 193.

"God, how things have changed (p. 130). Corti, *op. cit.*, p. 49.

"... even to his last drop of blood (p. 131). See Berghoeffer, p. 79.

"... unless they have to give way to violence (p. 131). Facsimile reproduced in G. Heuberger (ed), *The Rothschilds, A European Family* (Catalogue of an Exhibition at the Frankfurt Jewish Museum), 1994, p. 31.

"... about 700,000 gulden (p. 132). See Sauer, *op. cit.*, p. 121, 125.

"... more than 1,000,000 gulden annually (p. 132). See Dietz, *Frankfurter Handelsgeschichte*, iv/2, p. 734.

"... he established a temporary branch-office in Hamburg (p. 134). Protocol of Rothschild's police investigation, 8 August 1809, Ozoby arkhiv, Moscow 637/1/4.

"... my day begins at 4 in the morning and is often not over by 10 at night (p. 135). L. Buderus von Carlshausen, *op. cit.*, p. 37.

"They had been unable to find anything incriminating in his books (p. 136). Berghoeffer, *op. cit.*, p. 90.

"[Dalberg] was well disposed towards the Landgrave and he seems to have had some business dealings with Rothschild in the past" (p. 136). See Dietz, *op. cit.*, vol. 3, p. 361.

"Prince of Princes! The Beloved of God! (p. 137). Quoted in E. Mayer, *Die Frankfurter Juden* (Frankfurt, 1960), p. 50.

"... protection against insults and libelous outrage (p. 137). Quoted in K. von Beaulieu-Marconnay, *Karl v. Dalberg und seine Zeit* Weimar 1879, ii, p. 117.

"to meet Jewry in a spirit of humane benevolence (p. 137). See Beaulieu-Marconnay, ii, p. 119.

". . . commended Rothschild to the French generals and ministers (p. 137). Berghoeffer, *op. cit.*, p. 80.

"approach Napoleon as a humble petitioner (p. 137). *Ibid.*

"For this reason he refused to be given priority (p. 138). Cohen, *op. cit.*, p. 25.

"Jewish obscurantism (p. 138). Frankfurt City archive, Uglb. A. 23 Nr. 64.

". . . like the ghost of a murdered mother continues to accompany Christianity (p. 138). Quoted in Ludwig Geiger, *Die Deutsche Literatur und die Juden* (Berlin, 1910), p. 22.

". . . entirely dependent on the 'unanimous, explicit and formal agreement' of the Christian citizenry (p. 139). Quoted in *Neue Stättigkeit und Schutzordnung der Judenschaft zu Frankfurt, deren Verfassung, Verwaltung, Rechte und Verbindlichkeiten betreffend, wie solche von Seiner jetzt glorreich regierenden Hoheit des soveränen Fürsten Primas der Rheinischen Confederation festgesetzt und sanktioniert worden ist* (Frankfurt, 1808). Five parts, 152 paragraphs: 1. Religion and synagogues; 2. Education and schools; 3. Communal institutions; 4. Homes, professions, commerce; 5. Behavior of Jews towards Christians and vice versa.

"Goethe, who maintained that Jews, like women, had no 'point d'honneur' (p. 139). Quoted in P. Arnsberg, *Die Geschichte der Frankfurter Juden* (Frankfurt, 1983), i. p. 127.

". . . treating this race as it is and as it will remain for some time (p. 139). Goethe to Bettina Brentano ("Briefwechsel mit einem Kinde") (Berlin, 1881), p. 124.

"They can't be worse than their oppressors (p. 139). Quoted in *Jüdisches Leben in Frankfurt, 1796–1818* (Frankfurt, 1988), ii, p. 7.

"The trade in English and colonial goods never flourished in Frankfurt so much as it did after the imposition of the French blockade (p. 140). Quoted in F. Bothe, *Geschichte der Stadt Frankfurt* (Frankfurt, 1913), p. 567.

"Therefore I advise you to keep the goods with you until further notice (p. 141). RAL T3/17, 4 November 1806.

"That's the best speculation to be made (p. 141). RAL XI/86/OA, 20 August 1807.

"I hope that we will have soon a general peace (p. 142). RAL T5/4, 8 July 1807.

". . . our transactions with Sweden and [?] will be ruined (p. 142). RAL, 21 March 1808.

"Can't you keep up a regular correspondence with me in a businesslike way, or will you give up business? (p. 142). RAL T3/19, 16 June 1807.

". . . if it had not been for Rothschild's devoted services (p. 142). See Rainer von Hessen, *Die Rothschilds, Beitrage zur Geschichte einer europaischen Familie*, Catalogue of an exhibition (Frankfurt, 1994), p. 32.

". . . dangerous disease (p. 143). Cohen, *op. cit.*, p. 33.

". . . someone, perhaps Dalberg himself, had intervened in their favour (p. 143). Ozoby arkhiv, Moscow 637/1/4.

"God be thanked for this! (p. 144). Quoted in Rainer von Hessen, *op. cit.*, pp. 32–33.

"Amschel wrote back to say that Calmann was needed elsewhere for 'the main business' (p. 145). RAL T27/47 (1808).

"Rotschild [sic] generally has papers with him (p. 146). Corti, *op. cit.*, p. 68.

". . . [if they] could be certain of receiving the necessary financial support (p. 147). Quoted by Rainer von Hessen, *op. cit.*, p. 33.

". . . insisted that Savagner's warrant be 'extremely limited' (p. 148). French police report, quoted in Edouard Demachy, *Les Rothschilds, un famille de financiers juifs au XIXe siecle* (Paris, 1896), p. 99.

"The surviving protocol . . . (p. 148). Ozoby arkhiv, Moscow 637/1/4.

". . . a double set of books (p. 151). Archives Nationales, Paris, F/7 (Police General).

". . . had not raised the slightest suspicion or mistrust (p. 151). Ozoby arkhiv, Moscow 637/1/4/vi.

"[Nathan] is established very profitably in London and the youngest [Jacob] is staying with him there (p. 152). Quoted in Corti, pp. 99–100.

". . . advance its interests as far as he may find feasible (p. 152). Ozoby arkhiv, Moscow 637/1/4/134AR.

". . . he would never have got anywhere (p. 153). RAL T/27/105, 9 September 1914.

". . . never paid a single gulden in interest (p. 153). Marburg State Archive, Best. Buderus v. Carlshausen, 30 September 1809.

"Your loving father Mayer Amschel Rothschild (p. 154). RAL T5/10, 15 November 1809.

". . . his elder sons drew up a new 'irrevocable' partnership agreement (p. 155). Text in Berghoeffer, p. 219ff.

". . . our dear and wise teacher (p. 156). RAL T5/175, 26 January 1817; T27/107 24 October 1814.

"Yours faithfully/Mayer Amschel Rothschild/whose signature will be/ A. M. Rothschild will sign/S. M. Rothschild will sign/C. M. Rothschild will sign (p. 157). Ozoby arkhiv, Moscow 637/1/5/3, copy in RAL RFamAD/2.

6. Towards Emancipation

". . . their political and moral culture was not yet equal to that of Christians" (p. 158). Frankfurt City Archive, Uglb. D. 62.

"It is always unjust to tie someone's hands and feet and then complain that he does not want to walk" (p. 158). Quoted in Geiger's *Zeitschrift für die Geschichte der Juden*, vol. v. p. 206.

". . . our whole Jewry will very gladly pay the charges [imposed on them] for the happiness to obtain equal rights" (p. 160). Facsimile in Egon Corti, *Der Aufstieg des Hauses Rothschild* (Leipzig, 1929), opposite p. 114.

"As of that date, the remaining 240,000 fl. in annual installments with 5% interest" (p. 160). Facsimile in R. Heuberger and H. Krohn, *Hinaus aus dem Ghetto . . .* (Frankfurt, 1988), p. 24.

"You are now a citizen!" (p. 161). RAL T27/65, 13 December 1811.

"All are filled with ardent desire to prove their availability to the State" (p. 162). *Sulamith*, 5/11.

"Although it costs a lot of money, and perhaps another 30 Carolin on my share, I thank God for it" (p. 162). *Ibid.*

". . . the end of the world was near" (p. 162). See F. Bothe, *Geschichte der Stadt Frankfurt*, p. 567.

"I like Jews only *en masse*; *en detail* I strictly avoid them" (p. 162). Wilhelm und Karoline von Humboldt, *Wilhelm und Karoline von Humboldt in ihren Briefen*, (Berlin, 1900), vol. v, p. 236.

"The Grand-Duke scarcely ever refuses him a request" (p. 162). Archives Nationales, Paris, F/7 6575 D. 2964.

". . . it cannot be concealed under the clothes as letters can" (p. 163). Quoted in Corti, *Rise of the House of Rothschild* (New York, 1928), p. 93.

". . . at the ruined northern end of the Judengasse, for 9,284 gulden" (p. 163). Ozoby Arkhiv, Moscow 637/1/5/3.

"I pray put your brother in mind that I desire him, always, to forward [to Frankfurt] every object which is able to give profit here" (p. 163). RAL T5/9, 29 October 1809.

". . . everything in conformity with your good taste" (p. 163). RAL T5/11, 11 February 1810.

"*History of the Finances of the Landgraves of Hesse-Kassel*" (p. 164). See Sauer, *op. cit.*, p. 118.

"enrich my by a million" (p. 164). RAL T/5/18.

"I go on writing, so as not to forget how to write, and walking in order to keep my legs moving" (p. 164). RAL T32/210/1, 19 September 1810.

"A man has to think before he acts. But after having thought matters over everything else has to be left to God" (p. 165). RAL T29/184 24 August 1814.

"This was the man who through industry founded a world power of finance" (p. 165). M. Belli-Gontard, *Lebens-Erinnerungen* (Frankfurt, 1872), p. 38.

"He was fined 19,348 francs . . ." (p. 166). Archives Nationales, Paris, F/7 6575.

"You will kindly convey to them my satisfaction and gratitude" (p. 166). See Corti, p. 91.

". . . terrible need of funds" (p. 166). See *The Dispatches of the Duke of Wellington during his various Campaigns* (London, 1837), vi, p. 374.

". . . *they did not know how to get it to Portugal. I undertook all that*" (p. 167). See Buxton, *op. cit.*, pp. 353–4.

". . . adopted and supported by a rich and powerful clan" (p. 168). See A. Muhlstein, *Baron James, The Rise of the French Rothschilds* (New York, n.d.), pp. 40–41.

". . . the blindness of ministers in London has gone that far" (p. 169). Quoted in Gille, vol.i, pp. 46–7.

"Orders went out to follow his every move" (p. 169). Archives Nationales, Paris, F/7 2964 Serie 2, Boulogne-Mayence.

"The police in Dunkirk requested his 'eloignement' (removal)" (p. 169). *Ibid*, F/7 6551; "J'ai l'honneur de proposer a Votre Excellence d'ordonner son eloignement, par le motifs que je viens d'exposer."

"He certainly dislikes the French, even though he feigns loyalty to the French government" (p. 170). *Ibid*, 3 March 1812 F/7 6575.

"Well, nobody gets anything for nothing" (p. 171). RAL T27/66.

"Many have been conscripted. Father has therefore to do his part" (p. 173). RAL T27/66, 5 March 1812.

"To please Dalberg he offered him a collection of '303 extraordinarily beautiful' pieces" (p. 173). Bavarian State Archive, Dalberg Papers, 25 August 1812.

". . . in the region of his wound" (p. 173). Cohen, p. 6.

". . . because of Jewish stupidity" (p. 173). RAL T27/244, 4 March 1870.

"Amschel, keep your brothers together and you will become the richest men in Germany" (p. 174). RAL T30/20, 12 January 1815.

". . . full of days, riches and honor" (p. 174). Chronicles I, 29:28.

Aftermath

". . . our freedoms in the present generation and in those to come" (p. 177). Quoted in A. Freimann, *Stammtafeln der Freiherrlichen Familie Rothschild* (Frankfurt, 1906), p. 51.

". . . dedicated to all friends of virtue" (p. 177). Cohen, *op. cit.*, p. 4.

"Mayer Amschel von Rothschild and his descendents of both sexes" (p. 178). RAL T27/273 Amschel to Salomon and Jakob, 4 June 1817.

". . . you are acting like a drunkard" (p. 178). RAL Ta/41, T29/54, T32/294/2.

". . . united, [with] a common till, we have to work together without quarrels" (p. 180). RAL T30/201.

". . . big diplomatic dinners but ate [kosher food] before, prepared by his own cook" (p. 180). Belli-Gontard, *op. cit.*, p. 39.

". . . a sketch by Rembrandt, with the

profile of an intelligent monkey"
(p. 180). See Jules Michelet, *Journal I*
(Paris, 1959), p. 458.

". . . a regular bother asking me about
getting married and writing to uncle
Salomon that I only waited till his death
to marry a Christian" (p. 180).
RAL T7/8.

". . . perhaps the greatest figure ever to
adorn the international capital markets,
greater even than J. P. Morgan and
Michael Milken in their primes" (p. 180).
See J. Buchan, *London Review of Books*,
28 April 1994.

"Jew Rothschild and his
fellow-Christian Baring!" (p. 180).
Byron, *Don Juan*, Canto xii, verse v.

"You are the general and we are your
lieutenants" (p. 180). RAL T109/10.

". . . take two chairs" (p. 181). Quoted
in Victor Rothschild, *Shadow of a Great
Man* (London 1982), p. 7.

". . . when you have got it it requires ten
times as much wit to keep it" (p. 181).
Quoted in Buxton, *op. cit.*, p. 354.

". . . the people, and not only the
Chosen People but all the other Peoples
of the world, bow and pay obeisance to
him" (p. 181). H. Heine über Ludwig
Boerne, *H. Heine's Samtliche Werke*
(Berlin, 1887), vol. vii, pp. 120–1.

". . . wrote a moving little piece about
her" (p. 182). H. C. Andersen, *Bilderbuch*

ohne Bilder (Frankfurt, 1900).

"At ninety-four, still lucid, Guttle spoke
of acquiring a second house in the
country" (p. 184). RAL T7/42, Hannah
to Lionel de Rothschild, 16 January
1847.

"The deepest well can run out of water"
(p. 184). Gontard, *op. cit.*, p. 283.

"She died aged ninety-six in 1849"
(p. 184). A list prepared after Guttle's
death in 1849 conveys an idea of the
modest contents of the house during her
lifetime. The following items were
sealed in the presence of heirs and
notaries:

    1 settee
    1 screen
    6 chairs
    various porcelain items
    1 bed side table in glass
    1 oval table
    1 mirror
    3 bedsteads and beds
    1 chest of drawers
    1 mirror
    2 vases
    1 settee
    1 fire screen
    3 armchairs
    6 chairs
    1 small table
    1 mirror and small table
    2 brown pendulum clocks
    1 sofa
    6 chairs

BIBLIOGRAPHY

This bibliography is not limited to the sources cited in the Notes.

C. Andersen, *Bilderbuch ohne Bilder* (Frankfurt, 1900)

P. Arnsberg, *Die Geschichte der Frankfurter Juden* (Frankfurt, 1983)

F. Backhaus (and E. Hass and J. Schuchard), *Meyer Amschel Rothschild in Kassel* (Kassel, 1994)

S. A. Behrends, *Der Einwohner in Frankfurt a.M. in Absicht auf seine Fruchtbarkeit, Mortalitat u.Gesundheit* (Frankfurt, 1771)

M. Belli-Gontard, *Lebenserrinerungen* (Frankfurt, 1872)

C. W. Berghoeffer, *Meyer Amschel Rothschild* (Frankfurt, 1922)

K. v. Beaulieu-Marconnay, *K. v. Dalberg und seine Zeit* (Weimar, 1879)

F. Bothe, *Geschichte der Stadt Frankfurt* (Frankfurt, 1913)

N. Boyle, *Goethe, The Poet and the Age* (Oxford and New York, 1992)

B. Brentano, *Briefwechsel mit einem Kinde* (Berlin, 1881)

T. F. Buxton (ed), *Memoirs of Sir Thomas Fowell Buxton Bt.* (London, 1848)

L. Buderus. v. Carlshausen, *The Life of a Hessian Public Official in Difficult Times* (Hessenland Montasschrift, 1931)

S. J. Cohen, *Musterhaftes Leben des verewigten Herrn Bankiers, Meyer Amschel Rothschild* (Frankfurt, 1813)

E. C. Corti, *The Rise of the House of Rothschild*, translated by Brian and Beatrix Lunn (New York, 1928)

E. Demachy, *Les Rothschilds, un famille de financiers juifs au XIX siècle* (Paris, 1896)

A. Dietz, *Frankfurter Handelsgeschichte* (Frankfurt, 1910)

R. Ehrenberg, *Grosse Vermögen. Die Fugger, Rothschild,* (Krupp Jena, 1925)

A. Freimann, *Stammtafeln der freiherl. Familie Rothschild* (Frankfurt, 1906)

L. Geiger, *Die Deutsche Literatur und die Juden* (Berlin, 1910)

Geigers Zeitschrift fur die Geschichte der Juden

B. Gille, *Histoire de la maison Rothschild* (Geneve, 1965)

J. W. Goethe, *Werke* (Stuttgart u.Leipzig, n.d.)

Goethe im Gesprach (Zurich, 1944)

J. W. Goethe, *Faust*, translated by Walter Arndt (New York, 1976)

H. Graetz, *Geschichte der Juden* (Frankfurt, n.d.)

F. Hegel, *Early Theological Writings*, translated by T. M. Knox (New York, 1961)

H. Heine, *Gesammelte Werke* (Berlin, n.d.)

H. Heine, *The Poetry and Prose of*, translated by A. Kramer (New York, 1959)

H. Heine, (Hugo Bieber, ed) *Confessio Judaica, Eine Auswahl* (Berlin, 1925)

R. v. Hessen, 'Kurfurst Wilhelm I von Hessen und M. A. Rothschild', in G. Heuberger (ed.), *The Rothschilds, A European Family* (Frankfurt, 1994)

A. Hobson, *Imperialism, A Study* (London, 1902)

W. and K. von Humbolt, *In ihren Briefen* (Berlin, 1900)

F. Kapp, *Der Soldatenhandel Deutscher Fursten nach Amerika, 1775–1783* (Berlin, 1864)

L. Karamazin, *Letters of a Russian Traveller, 1780–90*, translated by F. Jonas (New York, 1957)

H. Karasek, *Der Fedtmilch Aufstand* (Frankfurt, 1969)

I. Kracauer, *Geschichte der Juden in Frankfurt (1150–1824)* (Frankfurt, 1925)

I. Kracauer, 'Frankfurt u. die Franzosische Republik', in Archiv fur Frankfurts Geschichte, 3. Folge.

I. Kracauer, *Geschichte der Judengasse, in Festschrift zur Jahrhundert* (Leipzig, 1874)

S. Krieg, *Frankfurter Burgerzwiste und Zustande im Mittelalter* (Frankfurt, 1864)

G. L. Kriegk, *Deutsche Kulturbilder aus dem 18. Jahrhundert* (Leipzig, 1874)

P. Losch, *Kurfurst Wilhelm I, Landgraf v. Hessen* (Marburg, 1923)

E. Meyer, *Die Frankfurter Juden* (Frankfurt, 1960)

J. Michelet, *Journal* (Paris, 1959)

A. Muhlstein, *Baron James, The Rise of the French Rothschilds* (New York, n.d.)

B. Muller, *Beschreibung des gegenwartigen Zustandes der Freien Reichstadt Frankfurt* (Leipzig, 1795)

Napoleon I, *Correspondence de* (Paris, 1863)

L. Poliakov, *Les Banquiers Juives et la Saint Siege du XIII au XVII siècle* (Paris, 1965)

L. Poliakov, *History of anti-Semitism*, translated by G. K. Littman (Oxford, 1985)

C. Ruhlig and Jurgen Steen, *Stadt u. Natur Frankfurt in 1780* (Frankfurt, 1982)

J. Sauer, *Die Finanzgeschafte der Landgrafen von Hessen-Kassel* (Fulda, 1930)

H. Schnee, *Die Hoffinanz und der moderne Staat* (Berlin, 1960)

H. Schnee, *Rothschild, Geschichte einer Finanzdynastie* (Gottingen, 1961)

S. J. Schroek, *Handlungsschema von Frankfurt* (Frankfurt, 1778)

J. J. Schudt, *Neue Franckfurter Judische Kleiderordnung* (Franckfurt am Mayn, 1716)

S. Stern, *The Court Jew* (Philadelphia, 1950)

Sulamith (Jewish Family Magazine) (Frankfurt, 1802–15)

N. Vehse, *Geschichte der deutschen Hofe* (Leipzig, 1911)

H. Voelker, *Die Stadt Goethes. Frankfurt im 18. Jahrhundert* (Frankfurt, 1932)

B. Williams, *The Making of Manchester Jewry, 1740–1875* (Manchester, 1985)

INDEX

Page numbers in bold denote caption and/or caption title